MOVEMENTS OF POWER

BOOKS BY BOB KLEIN

MOVEMENTS OF MAGIC, The Spirit of T'ai-chi-Ch'uan:
T'AI-CHI BODY-MIND MASTERY SERIES, VOL. I

MOVEMENTS OF POWER, Ancient Secrets of Unleashing Instinctual Vitality:
T'AI-CHI BODY-MIND MASTERY SERIES, VOL. II

T'AI-CHI BODY-MIND MASTERY SERIES
VOLUME II

MOVEMENTS OF POWER

Ancient Secrets of Unleashing Instinctual Vitality

Bob Klein

NEWCASTLE PUBLISHING CO., INC.
North Hollywood, California
1990

Edited by J. Kelley Younger
Copyedited by Ann McCarthy
Cover design by Riley K. Smith

This book is not intended to diagnose, prescribe, or treat any ail-
ment, nor is it intended in any way as a replacement for medical
consultation when needed. The author and publishers of this book
do not guarantee the efficacy of any of the methods herein described, and strongly suggest that at the first suspicion of any disease or disorder the reader consult a physician.

A NEWCASTLE BOOK

First Printing

    3   4   5   6   7   8   9   10

Printed in the United States of America

The following publisher has generously given permission to use
extended quotations from copyrighted work: *The Gospel of Truth*.
Copyright 1977 by Harper & Row. Reprinted by permission of the
publisher, Harper & Row.

This book is dedicated to you, the reader.

TABLE OF CONTENTS

INTRODUCTION

Did you, as a child, feel that you did not fit into the world around you, that you were born into the middle of a conversation and you didn't know what the conversation was about? Did you assume that everyone around you *did* know, and then spend considerable effort trying to understand that conversation so you could join in?

Perhaps, you thought, someday somebody will come to you and explain what's going on. He will tell you who you *really* are. His words will serve to remind you of your true nature and you will remember. And then you will understand what has happened to the world around you.

For now, you are only biding time, performing according to the rules you gleaned by watching those around you. You are living out your life and hope that sometime, hopefully before you die, someone will allow you or teach you to remember.

And how will you know this person? He or she may even walk right up to you and reveal all the knowledge you ever wanted to know, but you may ignore the experience because you don't recognize the teacher or the words.

Will you know the person by looking into his eyes? Will the eyes cause an effect in you which will make everything clear? Or will it be in his words and clever phrases?

This teacher will simply be a person who "remembers." So he will deal with you as he sees you on that level. In other words, his manner of interaction with you will reveal to you who you are. You will see a possibility of how people can relate to each other.

Don't we know a lot about ourselves by how others react to us? This can lead to a dependence on other people's level of awareness, in order for us to develop our own self-image. A teacher would cut through that dependence by talking directly to that which lies underneath your created self-image. Your knowledge of yourself will begin to come from your own direct awareness rather than from the limited awareness of others. A vibrant joy will begin to grow inside you.

When you know your real nature, you are happy. And when you can share that with another person, you are ecstatic. We can share, you and I. In fact, I am already happy because I'm now writing this book and sharing with you. I'm being your friend right now, long before you even knew it. And I can imagine myself reaching out to you (whoever you are) with these words, as two friends sitting on a bench in a park, enjoying each other's company.

In this book are some things I've found out in this life, things that seem very important. And I hope you, too, have found out some things and can share them with me. If a whole bunch of us got together and compared notes, we surely would have some spicy information.

I began this discussion in my earlier book, *Movements of Magic, The Spirit of T'ai-chi-Ch'uan*, and this volume is a continuation. I received many letters as a result of the first book. These letters constitute the other end of the conversation. In fact, I have spoken with people over the phone and met many wonderful people since that book was published.

Basically, they say that they had indeed already "known" the information contained in it. They had known these things since they were children. But they never spoke about them to anyone.

Perhaps they just didn't have the words. Or, they may have met with unpleasant reactions when trying to discuss their feelings with others. But they said that if they ever wrote a book, it would be the one I wrote.

Of course, I don't know any more than you do. We are all living, sensing beings. We are part of life and fully capable of perceiving the most intricate aspects of life. Yet we live in a society that is not based on promoting this awareness.

It's hard to maintain your awareness when you live in a society based on trapping your attention. We have developed that art to an extraordinary degree.

I've found that T'ai-chi-Ch'uan is a discipline that trains you to avoid the traps and to perceive your original, biological and "spiritual" heritage.

Don't worry about the word "spiritual." It simply means "the dynamics of attention," for attention is central to how we live our lives. The quality of attention itself will determine the quality of your life.

There is a training system to develop and channel attention, a system I have devoted much of my life to preserve. It is called "spirit breathing" and is described in this book. The term "spirit" as used here does not refer to ghosts or any such thing, but to your inner spirit, the quality of your being.

Even understanding that there *is* such a force as attention, which can be perceived, and that this force can be altered so that it has different qualities, is revealing.

Imagination is part of the process of perception, not merely the making up of something that is not there. Think what we do to ourselves, what we sacrifice, when we banish our creativity to certain small, isolated realms of our attention.

Attention is the land. Creativity is the king. And as it is said in the King Arthur tales, "The king and the land are one."

The human race began a huge experiment many years ago. It was the development of the human mind. The mind turned out to be the greatest tool and creativity was the craftsman that shaped it.

Yet something has happened. The mind has become stiff, brittle. It is not as resilient and absorptive anymore. The "king" has become like King Haggard in *The Last Unicorn*, by Peter Beagle (Ballentine Books, 1968), a dried-up shell of a person in a desolate land. Haggard trapped almost all the unicorns for his pleasure, but both he and his land became desolate.

Our minds have done the same. The mind has become dictator instead of benevolent king.

The land must be revitalized. Let us release the sureness of all things we "know" to be "absolutely true." Let us not use belief as if it were a weapon, used to defend one's life. Let us experiment with belief. Allow it to wander. Release your attention from "belief." Allow it to wander all over "feeling." Allow it to wander in the visual or auditory or olfactory world around you.

Let creativity become a messenger, calling to all the inhabitants of your "land," telling them about each other, encouraging and facilitating trade and communication among them. Is this not what a true leader does?

Creativity will flow once more all over the land. It will revitalize the land as true love revitalizes the soul.

These ideas take time to absorb. They are not so many facts to be stored in the memory banks, but rather, descriptions of experiences. Perhaps you would describe the same experience in a different way. But you undoubtedly know what I am talking about. You may say, "Oh, sure, isn't what you're talking about such-and-such a thing?"

One of my students is a plumber. No matter how lofty and poetic I get in describing something, he says, "Oh, sure, isn't that . . . ?" and describes it in the most basic terms—sinks, pipes, leaking faucets, etc. "Right," I say, "That's exactly what I'm talking about." We each relate to such matters in a different way, but we know what we are talking about.

When you recognize something I discuss, see how I explain it. Then determine how you would explain it. This book also tells how the Gnostics of the ancient Middle East explained it. You will probably find that, while the words and "beliefs" may differ, the experiences behind them are the same. For me, that is the magic and the power of T'ai-chi-Ch'uan.

—Robert Klein

Sound Beach, New York
June 1989

SECTION I

Understanding Hidden Teachings

CHAPTER 1
THE BOY AND THE EAGLE

T'ai-chi-Ch'uan and related disciplines are often called "mysterious," and to some, much of T'ai-chi's appeal is based on what we don't know about it. If it were widely known to be simple, understandable and, heaven forbid, even useful, it might lose its appeal for some people. Enrollment in T'ai-chi schools would drop and the remaining students might stop worshipping their teachers and instead look within themselves for the answers.

Faced with true understanding, students might be forced to expend "effort" and have to think for themselves! Then we teachers might be forced to stop conveniently repeating phrases we read from a book, and actually have to explain what T'ai-chi is about.

A dismal prospect, indeed. As my contribution to encouraging such a "dismal" future, this book is designed to remove the "mystery" in a way that makes all that can be gained from T'ai-chi both non-threatening and useful. We can use the analytical mind to get more than appears on the surface. Then we can get to the "meat" of the subject.

This is essential in studying any discipline. There is much "meat" encoded in the practice but you must learn to find it yourself. Then T'ai-chi will teach you directly and your teacher will become only a guide.

There are two pieces of writing I find useful in instructing students. The first is a simple children's tale I wrote as part of a children's series (not yet published). The second is a beautiful segment of Gnostic writing from some two thousand years ago. I include both of these in my "Master Healing Course," which delves into the healing systems of ancient tribal cultures and early civilizations. Much of my writing derives from such ancient material modified so there is at least a semblance of logic and order.

Here is the children's story, which holds lessons similar to those in T'ai-chi.

The Boy and the Eagle

In the land of clouds lived two spirits, Gene and Jody. It was time for both to travel to the world below.

But neither Gene nor Jody could decide what they wanted to be in the world called "Earth."

"I would love to become an eagle," said Gene, "but I would like to become a human, too!"

Jody said, "I would also like to become both an eagle and a human."

But a spirit cannot be both things at once. So they floated up to the highest cloud, to the "Giver of Form." Gene explained their problem to the Giver.

"I have heard so many problems in all my years. Yours is a simple one," he said. "Gene, you will become an eagle, and Jody will become a human boy. Live your lives for a few years and then change places. You, Jody, will go into the body of the eagle and Gene will go into the body of the human boy.

"I will put Gene in charge of making the change. This is because it is easy for a human to forget his spirit nature. An eagle never forgets."

"But how will I know when to make the switch?" Gene asked.

"You will know," said the Giver of Form. "I assure you, you will know."

Jody practiced with his new bow and arrows every chance he could get. But now his father called him to the teepee.

"You grow too old to play with the children. Our family needs meat and you are certainly old enough to catch some rabbits or quail."

Jody's mother stopped painting her beads. She looked at her husband with a proud face. Her boy was now a man. This is what the father really said: Jody, only ten years old, was now a man.

"My own child," she said, "soon will have the heart of an eagle."

He would have more than the heart of an eagle. He would have the feathers to wear in his hair and the claws and beak for a necklace.

Only one special eagle would do. It was born on the same day as Jody. When Jody walked in the hills, it followed him. When he rested, this special eagle perched on a branch and the boy watched him.

Jody felt something for this eagle. He would have it!

Early in the morning, a mist rose from the mountain lake. Jody knew the eagle would be there, perched on a high branch. He waited, bow in hand, for his prize to approach.

Gene looked down at his friend and was puzzled to see this thing in

Jody's hands. But the great eagle soon recognized the bow and arrow. This was the thing that had taken many of his friends' lives. It was a weapon of killing. And it was aimed at him.

Gene watched Jody pull back the string. He watched Jody take aim.

Gene thought, "When, if not now?"

A great wind carried Jody high into the air. He was thrown onto a high branch.

Jody blinked to clean his eyes of dust and then looked down to see —himself! He, Jody, now the great eagle looking down at Gene, now the boy. Gene, with a bow and arrow aimed at Jody.

The eagle remembered and let out a loud cry, "I am a spirit."

A great eagle soared high in the sky as Gene returned to his village. He entered his father's teepee. "I am an eagle," he explained to his parents. "I am a spirit."

His father replied, "Now you are truly a man."

Understanding the Story

Gene and Jody are two aspects of every person. In this story, the boy is not a monolithic being but an interplay of parts, each with its own will. This is how a mythological story is written. Such stories allow us to understand ourselves better, just as T'ai-chi does through movement.

In this case, there are two "parts." Throughout life, we are faced with the interaction of competing desires, wills, etc., and we try to keep it all coherent, to feel we are a unified "self." There is a Zen saying, "If everything returns to the one, to where does the one return?" Zen teaches its lessons through these short questions, or koans.

Gene was to become the spirit nature—that is, the part connected to nature, the part watching the antics of Jody, a boy concerned with status and human affairs. Jody sought to acquire the eagle by capturing it physically, just as we seek fulfillment in acquiring things.

In order to do this, he had to kill his spirit nature by shooting the eagle. And then, what would he really have—a few more trinkets!

Originally he had wanted to experience being an eagle. It was this desire, in the back of his heart, that expressed itself in the only way he knew—owning objects that represented his spirit side.

Gene watched as Jody pulled back his arrow. How often do we take aim at ourselves by berating ourselves or by carrying around anger which eats us up? The arrow represents the ways we hurt ourselves, including addictive habits.

But there is always something within us that knows the way out of this dilemma, and that "something" is strengthened by the practice of T'ai-chi.

When, If Not Now?

That "something" need only call for a change, make a commitment.

And when will that change take place? There is always an excuse to put it off. Yet the arrow is pulled farther and farther back. When will we join that T'ai-chi class? When will we practice our Form?

"When, if not now?" That question is valid at any moment in our lives.

And when we say, "Now," a great wind carries us up to a high branch so we can see from a better vantage point how we have been hurting ourselves.

Our spirit nature has been learning all this time and so has our human nature. They blend and mix and take advantage of each other's viewpoints. The internal battle ends.

The eagle/human flies high in the air. The human/eagle returns to the teepee. When Gene went home to the teepee and declared himself a spirit/eagle, his father responded that he was now truly a man. His father recognized the change that had taken place and explained that this change is necessary in the process of growing up into a man or woman.

His father understood that both Gene and Jody were his son and that an eagle claw necklace could only represent that change to adulthood.

Encoded Lessons

This is a story for children, yet it contains "information" which many adults might benefit from. Most good children's stories embody these lessons and are designed to be read repeatedly for many years until the child truly understands them.

In my particular style, I leave the ending somewhat unresolved. True, the switch was made and Gene was not killed. But the last sentence, "His father replied, 'Now, you are truly a man,'" still leaves some questions unresolved. Can't his father tell that it is now Gene, not Jody? And why did his father say that—simply because Gene declared himself to be an eagle/spirit?

The resolution is supposed to take place in the child's heart as he gradually understands the story's inner meaning. And this can only take place as the child gains life experience and the parent uses this story to help the child through these experiences. The resolution of the story is therefore the child's life itself. All my children's stories are designed this way and as I understand it, so are most children's teaching stories.

If you find such unresolved statements in this book, that would be a clue to dig a little deeper. In this way, you will feel that the "information" you gain is truly your own.

CHAPTER 2
ANCIENT GNOSTIC TEACHINGS AND T'AI-CHI-CH'UAN

In a sense, even non-fiction is a story. All writing paints a picture from a particular angle no matter how many "facts" may be listed. Some people don't put any effort into reading and merely accept whatever is in print without a critical eye. They use reading to add to their list of facts and assume that when a critical-minimum mass of facts is reached, they will be wise.

This absolves the reader of responsibility. Books like *Movements of Magic* and *Movements of Power* require readers to be responsible, to allow the words to affect them, and tune their attention inward to witness the effects. Then such a book can act as a searchlight, penetrating a usually dark and inaccessible area.

The Gnostics of old wrote with an eloquence that will always humble me as a writer. They were the student descendants of James, Peter and Thomas, the only disciples to be taught Jesus's inner teachings. Though not a Christian myself, I admire these writings and can think of no better volume to illustrate my points than *The Gospel of Truth* (from "The Nag Hammadi Library," Harper & Row, 1977).

The teachings emerging from these disciples are quite different from those of the Catholic Church, which may be why, around 300 A.D., the early church tried to kill all the Gnostics it could. Faced with extermination, the Gnostics buried their manuscripts to preserve them, knowing such manuscripts would likely meet a similar fate as the Gnostics themselves.

There are Gnostics today, their traditions having been handed down through the generations. Those I've met have explained that they were never quite sure whether those traditional teachings had been maintained accurately. Then recently, a buried treasure of Gnostic texts were unearthed at Nag Hammadi, in Egypt, and translated, reassuring present-day Gnostics.

T'ai-chi teaches lessons similar to those of the Gnostics, but through movement rather than through words.

Here are selections from *The Gospel of Truth*.

The Fashioned Creature

> Indeed the   all went about searching for the one from whom it had come forth, and the all was inside of him, the incomprehensible, inconceivable one who is superior to every thought. Ignorance of the Father brought about anguish and terror. And the anguish grew solid like a fog so that no one was able to see. For this reason error became powerful; it fashioned its own matter foolishly, not having known the truth. It set about making a creature, with (all its) might preparing, in beauty, the substitute for the truth. (*The Gospel of Truth*: 38)

When we are plopped into this world, we experience a multitude of sensations and experiences (the "all"), which Buddhists call "the Ten Thousand Things." More specifically, this term refers to the actions of our thinking-mind on our experiences, to create a "fashioned world." This paragraph is saying that there is a natural tendency for all these seemingly chaotic experiences to seek cohesion, that is, the feeling of an individual center linking all the experiences into a meaningful whole. We can see this in Sherlock Holmes stories. This crafty sleuth gathers little bits and pieces of information and works to organize some sense out of them.

In our own lives, by witnessing our perceptions and our reactions to those perceptions, we gradually come to understand who we are. Or at least, we have an impression of there being a single individual behind all this.

This individual is not a thought, an opinion, the senses, the emotions, etc., but is what lies behind all these things. It is incomprehensible, for whatever we can comprehend is a product of our thinking and comprehending; it is not the thinking and comprehending process itself.

A lack of self-knowledge leads to anguish, as with someone who has amnesia. Our life is not cohesive. We don't know what to expect of ourselves.

The Beautiful Creature

There are two solutions to this problem. One is to develop true self-awareness. The other is to craft an image of a person (a "creature") with a set of opinions, beliefs, behaviors, and so forth. The paragraph suggests that most people choose to "make a creature" which they call "me" and then try to make that creature as powerful as they can, by giving it the "correct" opinions—the most "beautiful" characteristics in the eyes of others. Yet this is only an image, just a substitute for the truth.

When we create a creature, beautifully fashioned with impressive thoughts, we come to depend on this creature and its powers for our happiness and success.

Yet the most beautiful creature in the world with the highest thoughts will not have any advantage over the least creature, when learning T'ai-chi. How many thoughts does a snake or eagle have, and yet how magnificently they move!

The mind tackles the T'ai-chi Form as an orderly sequence of movements which it can remember. But soon the student realizes that he must also remember whether to breathe in or out for each movement, and he must be aware of the direction and actions of several flows of momentum within the body created by the movements. There is too much for the mind to think about all at once.

Body-mind, Thinking-mind

Normally when we speak of the "mind," we are referring to what I distinguish as the "thinking-mind."

The thinking-mind is a singular fashioned creature. Its dynamics are singular in that it can concentrate on only one thing at a time. For the student to learn T'ai-chi, he must call on the part of himself that is comfortable and can work with the multiplicity of real life, the body-mind. This inner being keeps all the cells and organs working in harmony. It can certainly concentrate on the twenty or thirty things needed for practicing T'ai-chi exercises, like the Form or Push Hands. But if the thinking-mind still functions while you are practicing the Form, a fog is created. The thinking process robs attention from body-mind.

There is a distinctly different feeling doing the Form when the mind is on or off. One of my students told me that, even though he felt good after doing the Form, he started thinking that he wasn't doing it well and so became frustrated. His body feelings were telling him that he was doing the Form very well because the body felt relaxed, connected and in tune. Yet the mind pointed out that a hand was in the wrong position during one particular movement. The weight was wrong on another, and so on.

It's fine for the mind to point out such things; that's its job. The problem comes when your mind berates you for not being perfect. The mind fogs the central issue—practicing a healthful exercise that will turn your life around for the better.

Many of us have this complaining mind. And why? We live in a competitive world where everyone is trying to get ahead of everyone else. This frantic attitude pervades our interpersonal relationships, the emotional pattern of television characters and even the relationship of our mind to the rest of our being. The mind whips the rest of ourselves as a master whips a slave to make it work harder.

The Gnostic paragraph suggests that, ". . . the all was inside of him . . . who is superior to every thought. Ignorance of the Father brought about anguish and terror. And the anguish grew solid like a fog, so no one was able to see."

To put it simply, my student's feelings were telling him that the body appreciated his doing the Form. Yet his thoughts had been fashioned as a negative master, whipping the slave. His mind threw a cloud of anguish around him, separating him from the beautiful feelings inside himself which were thanking him for doing the Form so well.

Our True Self

The paragraph calls the Father ". . . incomprehensible, inconceivable . . ." The source of your existence, your true self, ". . . the one from whom it had come forth . . ." cannot be pinpointed or dissected out of your total experiences. The mind loves to pinpoint, to give an object a name and say, "That's what it is."

But our true self created all that we experience. It *is* all that we experience. The interplay of yin/yang is all that we know. That interplay is us.

And so, we can only know it, know our true selves, know the "Father," from our direct experiences. The mind is only a commentary on those experiences. It is really just another member of the community of experiences, not a master.

Taoist magic does not lie in commentary (in a "magic word," for example). It lies in the experience (in being part of life itself).

When a commentary seems to tell you what you are seeing, then you are surely living in a fog. As the chief said in the movie *The Emerald Forest*, "When a dream becomes flesh, trouble is not far behind." Or, as *The Gospel of Truth* says, "error . . . fashioned its own matter. . . ."

Echo of Expectation

How does the mind fashion its own matter? Such matter is like an echo. An echo is a sound bouncing off a wall. We look to the wall from which the sound seemed to have come, but we find nothing. And then we are confused.

Our lives are run to a large extent by what I call the "echo of expectation." Our minds tell us what we should expect to experience, what is or is not possible to experience, as learned from our society. Whatever our experiences may actually be, we only perceive them if they fall within a "possible" category.

I remember an "Amos and Andy" television show where the Kingfish was given an intelligence test. He had to fit a round peg into a round hole and a square peg into a square hole. When the square peg didn't fit into the round hole, he took out his pocketknife and chipped away the edges so it would fit. An echo of expectation is similar to that process.

Getting back to my student, his mind couldn't "know" the Form because T'ai-chi is a body-mind experience. So the mind told him that since it hadn't learned the Form well, the student himself hadn't learned it. I simply pointed out to him that it is another part of himself that learned it, a true, valid part of himself. His attention had to be directed inward, to that from which he ". . . had come forth . . ."

How loudly does the body have to thank you before you will say, "You're welcome"?

In Peter Beagle's *The Last Unicorn*, a skeleton watches as the wizard turns water into wine.

"Do it over here," he begs, "I can't see a thing." The mind always wants to know what's going on. When the skeleton drinks the wine, the wizard reminds him that the skeleton can't taste anything because he's dead. "Oh, but I remember!" says the skeleton, as his cheekbones glow red.

The mind wants to stick its nose into everyone's business, yet it cannot taste of life. It can only remember events and facts.

Clever manipulation of thoughts will not lead you to life, only looking inward and outward at the same time, and watching the process of creativity.

As you can see, this Gnostic writing deals with the same subject as T'ai-chi, the harmony of mind, body and nature. The Gnostic God is not some all-powerful monster in space but our true nature, the energy of creativity which Taoists call "Tao."

These teachings are practical guides to growing up as true human beings, and how they have been warped and misunderstood!

CHAPTER 3
THE LIVING BOOK

After all these, there came the little children also, those to whom the knowledge of the Father belongs. Having been strengthened, they learned about the impressions of the Father. They knew, they were known; they were glorified, they glorified. There was revealed in their heart the living book of the living—the one written in the thought and the mind (of the) Father, and which from before the foundation of the all was within the incomprehensible (parts) of him—that (book) which no one was able to take since it is reserved for the one who will take it and will be slain. No one could have appeared among those who believed in salvation unless that book had intervened. For this reason the merciful one, the faithful one, Jesus, was patient in accepting sufferings until he took that book, since he knows that his death is life for many. (*The Gospel of Truth*: 39)

(Note that a dash (—) represents a lost piece of the scroll.)

Little children are not yet caught up in the game of "making creatures" or images. They *are* creatures (though programming may start very early).

I remember being resentful whenever someone came to a conclusion about what kind of person I was, because this trapped me into the image-making game. They were trying to fashion my image instead of accepting my variability and my growth. People love to fix another person (and themselves) into a simple, understandable pattern.

Young children to some degree are still directly connected to earth, to their biological creaturehood, rather than their mental/social creaturehood. Their body-minds are active in the world. Their true selves and their social roles (their play) are not so far apart. "They knew, they were known. . . ." They are aware of themselves, and can recognize when someone else is being himself or acting a role or an image instead.

Losing Yourself

I remember that I felt (as do many people) that my real self was not known by others. They knew only their image of me. My true feelings faced a serious, cold world that allowed only acting. I began acting to survive and can remember feeling lonely for the me I used to know but had little time or opportunity to express (until I found other "kindred spirits").

It seemed that I was born into the middle of a conversation and everyone knew what it was about, except me. Then I realized that this "conversation" wasn't about anything real. It was just programmed, repetitive behavior. If you joined in, it showed you were a member of the "clan," as long as your opinions and feelings were "correct."

Women seem especially prone to this problem. Perhaps because of their up-bringing, they don't feel they "should" speak up for their real needs and feelings but should have just the "proper" ones. There is a tremendous (destructive) force to be "proper." Soon, the true self is forgotten, but it always feels anguish. It is unknown to others and to itself. There is no glory or joy in life, because that which is glorified and is grabbing for joy is not oneself but a fashioned creature. So even if glory and good tidings come your way, it is not really "you" who enjoys it. The true self sighs. And the heart sinks.

A book is filled with knowledge. But this paragraph mentions a "living book of the living" which is revealed in the heart. It is not a written book but an inner knowledge, which is biological in nature. For this book was written ". . . from before the foundation of the all was within the incomprehensible (parts) of him . . ." It is the knowledge of nature herself at work and of the creature of truth, that is, your real self. It is not a book filled with the clever knowledge the mind can think up.

Rebirth

The living book is only accessible to one who will ". . . take it and will be slain." When you experience your real self, then the fashioned self—the one you spent your life creating—seems so foolish. The very moment you know yourself, the fashioned creature is slain. It no longer can create the illusion, the fog around the real you. This is because now you know what the real you is.

For example, the mind may capture your attention all your life with its ramblings. It may convince you that what it has to say is important. Should you gain the courage to pay attention to something else (such as your T'ai-chi practice), it will say, "Wait a minute! Wait till you hear what I've got to say next!"

So the inner, living book is for those who will reply, "Oh? Wait till you see what I'm going to *do* next!"

There is a beautiful Zen story of the master who calls in his head student. The master is old and is giving control of the monastery to the student. The master takes out a notebook containing all of his wisdom and hands it to the student, whereupon the student throws the notebook into the fire. "What are you doing!" shouts the master. "What are you saying?" replies the student. Zen is a teaching beyond words.

To let go of all you've invested in that fashioned creature and allow the attention to seep into the biological self is a death and re-birth. We never lose the fashioned creature. We only lose our addiction to it.

Children, of course, understanding their fashioned selves as play, do not undergo such a death for they have not yet been fooled into thinking that the phantom creature is really alive.

The paragraph suggests that all spiritual growth comes from an awareness of oneself.

Fashioned Creature as Actor

Let's take what *The Gospel of Truth* has to say about Jesus and use it, not as the historical Jesus, but as a metaphor for this process of inner growth. Let us say that Jesus is the son of God—that is, a product or personality created from the true self but one that is aware of its source.

Such a creature deals with worldly affairs yet is still connected to itself. It knows that the "slings and arrows of outrageous fortune" are the sufferings of the phantom, not of the Father, the true self. So it knows that the death of the phantom (that image that tries to bind and solidify all our experiences into a single imagined being) is life and freedom for our entire complex of living experience.

In this state, each experience, each perception, each new day is a life form of its own and is allowed its independence. It is not choked off, relevant only as part of an imagined person with strict, pre-set, patterned behavior. The creature that knows the Father, understands that its death ". . . is life for the many."

Winning and Losing

There is a similar slaying that takes place in T'ai-chi. The initial motivation for learning is often to win something. You may want to win good health, respect, the ability to protect yourself, or enlightenment.

For example, when you begin Push Hands, you want to push your partner more than he pushes you. Your motivation is being better than the next student. Yet that very attitude prevents you from merging with the partner, which is the only way to do Push Hands successfully.

I visited one school where the partner slapped me on the shoulders whenever I pushed him, as if to say, "How dare you!" I was very surprised but no one else seemed to think anything of it. As I practiced with each student I noticed that they all did the same thing. It certainly was not a push; it was a sort of retaliation. Since my eyes are closed while doing Push Hands, I thought this was an especially rude thing to do, but I didn't say anything. These students seemed to be practicing T'ai-chi to reinforce their fashioned creatures, rather than to discover the living book of the living.

The feeling of two isolated individuals attempting to defeat each other must be transformed into a feeling of harmonizing the two individuals into a single creature composed of flows of energy.

The Play of Individuality

To allow this, you must be willing to let go of your individuality in order to merge, on the one hand, while on the other hand, to maintain a form of separateness that allows an interplay between two different wills. Thus, you are recreating the wholeness of the yin/yang, but on a much more complex level.

To illustrate more intimately this idea of being slain, take the case of two lovers. Being slain refers to the way, when being affectionate, one may take the liberty of manipulating the lover's position, for example, without asking for permission. In love, the individuality dissolves to some extent and one partner loves to see the other taking liberties with his or her individuality. Allowing the individuality to be slain and each will to be happily taken over by the other is an essential part of affection. Otherwise, you are walking on eggshells, which leads to an unpleasant relationship.

Yet, the individuals remain intact. There are those who fear to let the protective wall of their wills be slain lest their individuality be lost. Push Hands helps them practice this play of separating/merging.

Being slain leads you to a deeper understanding of yourself, beyond defending your individuality. Once you learn to merge with a Push Hands partner, you can merge the separate parts of yourself, so the mind no longer wars with the body-mind.

It allows you to sacrifice for the betterment of a community or earth.

Push Hands is certainly not for the sole purpose of learning how to push people. Encoded in its movements are principles as important to our lives as you will find anywhere.

Teachings that Are Beaten into You

Nowhere is this teaching of being slain carried to such a degree as in T'ai-chi kickboxing. The beginning student is tense and angers easily. He doesn't want his partner getting the better of him. Soon he realizes that no matter how skilled he may be, some punches and kicks will come through. He may even be injured from time to time.

The more tense he becomes, the slower his reactions and the more he gets hit. He can then realize that the tension, associated with the competitive feeling, is what allows his partner to beat his head in. His mind, which is offended by being hit, gets angry. His body knows he must stay loose to survive.

So there you have it. The mind causes the body to get beaten up because of its easily offended nature. How often do we make decisions based on our ego rather than on our real needs?

Luckily for the T'ai-chi student, his body can only take a limited amount of pounding. At some point the body will tell the mind to keep its offended sensitivities to itself. And the body will loosen up in order to survive. This is a perfect example of a death and re-birth. The student has gained an inner knowledge in exchange for being slain (not by his partner but rather by not identifying so much with the mind's sensitivities).

One student told me he was startled by the fact that I smiled when I fought. He thought either that I was sadistic or that there was something he didn't understand about fighting. It took him only a few months to understand. Whenever he became especially offended, I laughed. This wasn't to be rude. It was because the situation was genuinely funny. How could he be offended by my teaching him how to protect himself?

Students often apologize when they land a punch on me. I have to assure them that this is the point of what they're doing.

At times, my gloves will loosen and I stop in the middle of fighting to adjust them. The student might not realize what I'm doing and punch me in the head. At first, the student will apologize but when he sees no reaction on my part, he realizes that his punches don't offend or hurt me. I continue adjusting my gloves with no regard for being punched.

Some students will go out of their way to punch me when I'm adjusting my gloves because that may be the only chance they get. And we laugh over it. Yet those punches are not just love taps, they are all-out punches.

The strange thing is that when you have learned to neutralize, even strong punches mean very little. William Chen used to let his students practice punching his face full force, one punch after another, until the students' wrists were sore. It was more disturbing to the students than to Grandmaster Chen.

In this way, the student is actually the one who is slain. That is, the student's attitude of isolation, of fearing to let his energy out to another, fearing to anger another, fearing to be spontaneous, is neutralized.

What once was intimidating is now funny. What once bound you to a false life, now opens you up to real life.

And strangely, the fighting students do not become aggressive in everyday life. This is because once fear is neutralized, anger is neutralized and so is destructive aggression.

The Repertoire of Feelings

The slow, relaxing Form is no less a place to be slain than the fighting. Its smooth, continuous movements are anathema to the mind, which jerks from one thought to another. Students will frequently tell me that they experienced this or that feeling while doing the Form, and ask what it means.

We call these the "repertoire of feelings," the living book of the living. Students may notice that they feel a certain way every time they come to a specific part of the Form. Each movement seems to be associated with a specific overall feeling.

Such feelings are the communication system of the body, much as thoughts are the communication system of the thinking-mind. The purpose of the mental communication system is to serve as your representative in society. The repertoire of feelings are thus described verbally. The steps from the homeostatic needs of the body (its need to maintain health) to verbal communication are as follows:

Step 1. The body's conditions are reflected in the repertoire of feelings.
Step 2. The repertoire of feelings is translated into ideas and words.
Step 3. The understanding of the person you're talking to is taken into consideration, so these ideas will make sense to that person. In this way, you are promoting your needs to the world around you.

Too often, the roles of the mental ideas and the repertoire of feelings are reversed. The person you are talking to or the book you are reading conveys an idea to your mind. Then your mind translates this into feelings to convince it of the needs of the world around you.

Obviously, this latter process is sometimes necessary. We cannot always have our own way. Both pathways need to remain open. Unfortunately, when the latter process is used exclusively, the body's needs are not only neglected but the body seems like a separate person. It is as if your own body is that other person who needs to be convinced, as in step 3 above. It would then be easy to convince you that you are not good enough, not enlightened enough, etc., and that some sort of philosophy or religion or other belief system is needed to make you good.

By working with the repertoire of feelings and expanding your attention all the way down to the cellular level so you can actually experience the body's cells at work, T'ai-chi reconnects you with yourself.

Someone once told me that the only purpose of the body is to carry around the mind. This would be an extreme case of the reversal of the natural process.

Out of the Cage

The next step after wanting to win in T'ai-chi is to want to become humble—to "win" humility you might say. Instead of desiring to overcome the opponent, you may want to not want to overcome him.

At this stage, a T'ai-chi student may wind up not caring about anything. He becomes listless. This pretentious humility is just as destructive as fighting battles of your own making.

So how do you win? How do you come out of a practice such as T'ai-chi a vibrant, non-combative, healthy, merged individual? This reminds me of the "Star Trek" episode in which a superior race locks Captain Kirk and Spock in an energy cage. They want to do an experiment on Spock but gave Kirk the choice as to which experiment they will perform.

To paraphrase the beings, "If we do the first experiment, Spock will have a high chance of dying. If we do the second, he will have an even higher chance of being brain-damaged. Which do you choose?"

Spock discovers that the energy cage they are in is powered by their own emotional excesses. (Or rather, by Kirk's emotional excesses, since Spock wouldn't have any.) By relaxing and calming their minds, the two heroes are able to simply walk out of the situation.

The trick is to understand the cage you are in, how you keep it energized, and when you stop energizing it, where you will walk to. It is all a matter of attention. The mind can be such an energy cage. T'ai-chi relaxes you and teaches how to sink your attention into every crevice of your experience so that once again, you fill your world. It is the drive to find the pot of gold, the ultimate singularity of happiness, within the mind, that keeps you caged.

My first T'ai-chi teacher described it this way: "There is no such thing as the ultimate pizza." We search for ultimate solutions but we search only within our echo of expectation. How do we escape from this echo?

Patience

The Gospel of Truth says, "No one could have appeared among those who believed in salvation unless that book [the living book] had intervened. For this reason . . . Jesus was patient in accepting sufferings until he took that book. . . ."

We T'ai-chi students must be patient as we make conscious our repertoire of feelings and truly become alive. The anxiousness of wanting to excel quickly and have some signs or symbols of our progress are our version of "sufferings." Such symbols are only for the satisfaction of our echo of expectation and tend to reinforce it.

One of my students engaged in repetitive behavior each time he greeted me or the other students. If we did not play our parts precisely, he felt we were not being friendly. I simply nodded when he did this and made sure not to play into that game. Then after a few months, I explained that the reason I remained distant was to allow him to feel the result, in his repertoire of feelings, of someone who absolutely resisted tying into his game. This was a necessary step in helping him to break his repetitiveness and allow him to become spontaneous. He told me he understood and appreciated what I had been doing, and asked, now that he knew, could I play into his games from now on. He used different words but the essence was that since his mind knew what I was doing, I should now stop doing it. No such luck. That would not have served him.

Allow the living book, the repertoire of feelings, to "intervene" and grow, and have faith that your daily practice will enrich your life. Then you can simply walk out of your cage.

Sitting on the Stone of Eternity

Another example of this principle was in a comic book I read as a child, called, I think, *Strange Tales*. The seeker finally was allowed to enter the inner chamber in which sat the guru, on a stone.

The guru, "impressed" by the seeker, allowed him to sit on the stone of wisdom, whereupon the guru got up and was about to leave. But he made one parting remark. To paraphrase, "I have been sitting on this stone for hundreds of years. I, too, was a seeker. And the guru who sat here before me told me that if I ever got up off that stone, I would immediately die, unless someone else took my place. Now I tell you the same thing."

The guru left and the seeker sat in anguish. If the guru was right, the seeker would have to sit in that one spot forever, until he could trick someone else into sitting on the stone. But if the story wasn't true, he could get up at any time and leave. And so the story ended. What a great description of life!

You, the reader, may be sitting on that stone right now. How would you decide? How *do* you decide? Your mind may be telling you that, should you get off that stone (your pattern of behavior, your self-image, even the act of thinking itself), you will die.

All these stories, from "Star Trek" to comics to the ancient Gnostic writings to T'ai-chi to a children's video, are useful in getting the point across. One is not better or more sacred than the other. Teachings and teachers are all around us. Yet how desperately we search for understanding!

By using everyday examples for such teachings, we can see that they are practical, simple, achievable and immediately available.

CHAPTER 4
BECOMING WHOLE

Each one's name comes to him. He who is to have knowledge in this manner knows where he comes from and where he is going. He knows as one who having become drunk has turned away from his drunkenness, (and) having returned to himself, has set right what are his own. He has brought many back from error. He has gone before them to their places, from which they had moved away when they received error, on account of the depth of the one who encircles all spaces while there is none that encircles him. It was a great wonder that they were in the Father, not knowing him, and (that) they were able to come forth by themselves, since they were unable to comprehend or to know the one in whom they were. If his will had not thus emerged from him—for he revealed it in view of a knowledge in which all its emanations concur. (*The Gospel of Truth*: 40)

Each of us is programmed to some extent with patterns of self-image (one's name). A Zen koan says, "Give your flesh back to your mother and your bones back to your father." *The Gospel of Truth* describes this as one who was drunk and turns away from drunkenness to ". . . set right what are his own."

Our fashioned creature is, to a large extent, fashioned by others. Let us assume that the "they" spoken of in this paragraph refers to the elements of our being, the living parts of our experience.

When read on another level, the world itself, along with all people, are the elements of "God's" being, the living parts of "God's" experience.

It doesn't really matter on which level this treatise is read. The same principles apply. But here, we are concerned with our own immediate, practical lives.

The student's real self ("He") remembers his original face, his being, the feeling of himself, before programming occurred. He becomes aware of his true feelings (". . . their places, from which they had moved away . . . .") rather than the feelings of the image he created.

Have you ever, in a particular situation, asked yourself what *should* you feel, what would be correct to feel? Then, realizing that you didn't actually feel that way, chastise yourself. You compare your true feelings with a predetermined list and find them wanting. In this case, you are not using your feelings as a gauge of the reality right in front of you.

It is said that a dog can sense whether someone has good or bad intentions and that we should pay attention to the dog's reactions. Yet we may not even pay attention to our own reactions. Has it come to a point where we need dogs to feel for us?

One of the aspects of T'ai-chi-Ch'uan is the shamanistic form of healing. The above paragraph of the *Gospel* gives a good foundation for understanding that methodology, which deals with your connection to nature.

Hints of the Garden of Eden

Have you ever been struck by a beautiful feeling, wafting through you like drifting smells from a bakery? You may have dismissed it as a passing feeling, the effects of a breeze or seeing something beautiful. It may have seemed like the hint of a garden of Eden within you.

The legends of a Garden of Eden, heaven, astral planes, and all sorts of mystical realms abound in literature or, perhaps, in our minds. There is such a land. You can reach it only one way. Just stop deceiving yourself. You do not reach this land by further perfecting the fashioned creature, but by un-fashioning it.

I went to the wedding of a couple who met at my school. A woman I had met only twice before came over to my table. She said she had just come to say hello and was glad to see me. That simple act was a reminder that the Garden of Eden is right here. It was in her kindness.

Another student of mine once told me he had a negative opinion of most people because they were "unaware, unspiritual beings." I told him a story from the Middle East that he realized applied to his situation. It goes like this:

> *Two men sat just outside of a city. A traveler approached and asked, "What kind of people can I expect to find in this city?" One of the men answered, "What kind of people were in the city you came from?" The traveler replied that there were horrible people where he had come from, thieves, murderers and all sorts of slime. "That's the same kind of people you will find here," said the man.*
>
> *Then another traveler came by and asked, "Sirs, can one of you tell me what sort of people I will find in this city?" The same man replied, "What kind of people live in the city you come from?"*
>
> *"Oh, they're wonderful people, always willing to help out their neighbors." The man told him, "Those are the same kind of people you will find here."*

When the second traveler had left, the friend of the man who had given the advice asked him how he could have given two different answers to the travelers. "You told one that he would find horrible people here, and to the other traveler you said he would find good people here."

The other man replied, "There are good people and bad people wherever you go. If you find mostly good or bad that is because you attract those people to you."

My student started being friendlier to the people he met in his new home of California. And another student of mine is starting to be friendly to people on his job.

The magic land is the very place you are now, without all the nonsense that comes from fashioning an image.

The Golden Image

In Judaism, you are not supposed to create an image of God. The symbolic example is of a golden calf or cow, but the meaning refers to your own self-image. Imagine a golden cow. A cow is a cow, right? Ah, but it's made of gold! Sometimes we can be cows made of gold.

We try to make our images shine but it is only an act. Thus, we divide ourselves from others, complain about them and point to ourselves as examples of what should be.

Yet what happens when you operate from your true self? You find that you are not really a single, individual thing sitting in the middle of a huge world. When you let go of the image, down to its core, you are left with the entirety of your experience. You can no longer point to this thing or that thing as yourself as if the rest were not part of you.

Jesus explained this process of letting go of the self-image very well when he described it metaphorically as the apocalypse, the second coming. It seems like your world is truly coming to an end, but then the sky lights up from one end to the other when you realize that the world which is coming to an end is built of your own self-delusion (covered with gold). It's like someone saying they love you and then lying to you. On the one hand you think to yourself that they did say they love you. But when you examine the situation a little further you begin to question anything they say.

But after awhile, you get used to such hypocrisy and, while you may not like it, you understand and accept it as a natural phenomenon. You realize that you make mistakes also, and just start watching yourself. Each event is a learning experience so you can know more about the world and stop using each event as an opportunity to complain. You can see what someone does and still love them. In this way, you stop separating yourself from other people or from the world around you.

Encircling All Spaces

You find that you encircle all spaces. You have great depth. You allow all your experience into your heart. There is no part of your awareness that is not you. No one thing can encircle your entire being.

This state does not make you an almighty, divine God-like being. You're the same flawed being as you always were but you identify with the world around you, rather than with just the separating, dividing, complaining mind.

It is a great wonder when you actually experience the world around you as yourself. According to a Zen saying, "The inside and outside are made of the same flesh." When this state of being is reached, then a "terrible" thing happens. There is nothing to be better than, and no one to accomplish that betterness and so you don't feel like complaining. Whatever you do for others you do for yourself as well.

It is a wonder how this state is reached, then, since there is no one to achieve this state. Or, as conveyed by *The Gospel of Truth*, these disparate experiences and sensations seem to join to a common identity and that common identity (your true identity) is experienced all at once: ". . . they were able to come forth by themselves . . . ," yet previously, ". . . they were unable to comprehend or to know the one in whom they were." It is a wonder!

". . . [A] knowledge in which all its emanations concur," is the recognition that all you experience is part of yourself and not outside you.

Responsibility of an Addict

This leads to responsibility, and worst of all, effort. You take *responsibility* for your life, for all the emanations, and put forth *effort* to be creative in your life. (I have found these two words to be abhorred by many people.)

When you end your battles (complaints) with the world around you, you find that the battles within you have ended as well. For the outside is the inside.

One of my teachers explained that many people love battles because being frantic causes the body to produce endorphins, natural chemicals that make us feel good, and are addictive. So they seek out negative situations in order to trigger these feelings. The "high" they experience is interpreted as spiritual or a "higher plane" of consciousness. It is as difficult for them to be around calm, balanced people as it is for a heroin addict to give up his drug.

Accepting the world around you as yourself is really a process of withdrawing from an addiction. The tension in our bodies is a reflection of our addiction to internal battles. Letting go of our addiction to the mind's programming (which causes these battles) can feel like the apocalypse.

The T'ai-chi Process

When a T'ai-chi student first begins learning the Form, he feels very awkward. The movements and position of every part of the body must be precise. All the details of the Form are the "emanations" of the Form.

But where do these emanations emanate from? At first, they come from the mind, which thinks about each position, each posture, etc. The Form is an emanation of the mind at this time.

The teacher can see the quality of the student's mind from his Form.

In the second stage of learning the Form, the student is advised to notice how each movement affects each part of the body—how the contraction of one muscle to move the hips, for example, requires that other muscles adjust to keep the body in balance.

The student becomes more and more aware of how all the parts of the body work with each other. The student's attention is then directed to the way breathing affects all the parts of the body. Then, how the nature of the surface of the ground affects all the above. Then, how the student's concentration affects all the above.

This goes on until every aspect of doing the Form is experienced as a living "community." This community is not necessarily directed by a single director (the "I") but is more like an interacting, cyclic ecosystem.

At this point, the teaching of imagery is brought in. The student is given a single experience. It can be feeling a piece of cloth, watching flowing water, chewing gum, watching a fluttering leaf—or really anything. (In our school, it is often handling snakes or staring into their eyes.) While doing the Form, the student concentrates on this experience and finds that the Form somehow becomes an expression of the experience.

Unpredictable Creativity

To truly accomplish this, the student must let go of his own self-image and replace that with the experience he is working on. This allows creativity to have more control than the rigid images the student has had programmed into him.

Creativity is unpredictable, spontaneous. Yet, as the student allows creativity to gain more power over his life, he finds that it has an intelligence, a wisdom and is meaningful. In fact, the intelligence of creativity is felt as a powerful force, permeating all of one's experience, while the activities of the mind seem to be barriers, fences, cages of the creativity. The mind serves to hold fast to a particular moment or pattern of creativity. The process of "letting go," so vital in T'ai-chi, allows creativity freer movement through one's life.

Letting go never seems safe, for who knows what the creativity will do? Safety is found in the mind while the vitality of life is found in creativity.

Working with imagery brings us back "to their places from which they had moved away." The mind takes a limited amount of the raw material of creativity and then fashions it into a fixed understanding. It values a pattern or understanding that remains fixed and unmoving, and calls it "truth."

Creativity however, values change and motion. Have you ever noticed how energetic you become when you are being creative? The balance of thinking-mind and body-mind, fixation and creativity, affects your whole being. The "Son of God" is one who has a good balance of the two.

Such a person has no problem learning because he is fluid enough to accept new ideas and has the ability to "fix" these new ideas in memory so they can be recalled easily.

Working with imagery in the Form teaches us this balance. Students often get the feeling that they have been there before, that they once experienced this practice of imagery long ago. That once upon a time, was before the thinking-mind gained more power than the free-flowing creativity. It was when you did not resist the world or place barriers between the various parts of your experiences.

Chi-gung, the teaching of the flow of chi, is designed in large part to address this problem. The barriers we create between "ourselves" and "our experiences" are reflected internally as blockages to the flow of chi (internal energy).

Called "spirit breathing" by many cultures since ancient times, Chi-gung re-connects us to the "Father," to the totality of our experience. The senses, body, mind, emotions, breath, gravity, momentum, will, attention, etc., re-join and re-form their original cooperative community.

Often taught as merely a series of breathing exercises, Chi-gung sobers us up from our drunkenness. There is a beautiful description of spirit breathing (the form of Chi-gung I teach) in the following paragraph:

> For the Father is gentle and in his will there are good things. He took cognizance of the things that are yours that you might find rest in them. For by the fruits does one take cognizance of the things that are yours because the children of the Father are his fragrance, for they are from the grace of his countenance. For this reason the Father loves his fragrance and manifests it in every place, and if it mixes with matter he gives his fragrance to the light and in his repose he causes it to surpass every form (and) every sound. For it is not the ears that smell the fragrance, but (it is) the breath that has the sense of smell and attracts the fragrance to itself and is submerged in the fragrance of the Father. It shelters it, then, takes it to the place where it came from, the first fragrance which is grown cold. It is something in a psychic form, being like cold water . . . which is on earth that is not solid, of which those who see it think it is earth; afterwards it dissolves again. If a breath draws it, it gets hot. The fragrances therefore that are cold are from the division. For this reason [faith] came; it did away with the division, and it brought the warm pleroma of love in order that the cold should not come again but there should be the unity of perfect thought. (*The Gospel of Truth*: 45)

This is not mystical writing. It is a clear description of what you can expect from your practice—clear landmarks and guidelines, and a clear description of the theory behind the practice.

". . . [T]he Father loves his fragrance. . . ." His energy flows out to that which He loves—to us and our world ("He," meaning your true self).

". . . [I]f it mixes with matter he gives his fragrance to the light. . . ." He allows his energy, his attention to merge with the world he senses around him.

". . . ([I]t is) the breath that has the sense of smell and attracts the fragrance to itself and is submerged in the fragrance of the Father." This shows that the chi (fragrance) is intimately associated with breath, which ". . . attracts the fragrance to itself . . ." The breath draws in chi.

"The fragrances therefore that are cold are from the division." However, "If a breath draws it, it gets hot." This gives an invaluable clue to you for the practice of spirit breathing.

The chi-invigorated breath takes the chi ". . . to the place where it came from . . . ," thus describing how Chi-gung is used to allow the release of creativity, the Father. The breath and chi fill every cell of the body so the communication systems are sensitized. Attention is decentralized and calmed so that the creativity flows through it like sound waves through water. If you get nothing more from this book than an understanding of the previous sentence, the whole book will have been worth reading.

Could it be possible that the Gnostics were Taoists? Or was there simply a free flow of ideas among cultures at that time? Or, are these principles so obvious that many cultures have come up with the same descriptions, the same kind of disciplines? Those questions are certainly a fertile ground for anthropological study, though beyond the scope of this book.

T'ai-chi spirit breathing begins with learning which are the in-breaths and which are the out-breaths in the Form. Then the student moves the focal point of his attention up the spine and out the top of the head on the in-breath and down the spine, down the legs and into the earth on the out-breath. This is done as a sitting meditation, a standing meditation and during the Form. It strengthens one of the basic flows of energy—heaven and earth.

In an advanced breathing technique, the flow of energy and attention goes both ways at once, creating a slightly taut pole or cord of energy in a line going through the body and down into the earth's center.

To reinforce this experience and tie it into a mythology, students at the school are brought through a guided imagery using an American Indian drum. This experience ("The Earth Initiation")[1] gives a vivid, personal and convincing experience of being connected to an intelligent planet.

Gravity Is the Attention of the Earth

The heaven/earth energy is directly in line with the direction of gravity. Gravity is the attention of the earth. It is useful to think about that idea for a moment.

Our attention is what connects us to the world around us. When we are

---

1. An audio cassette of this guided imagery is available from Artistic Video (see last pages).

really paying attention to something (as in love), we are oblivious to everything else. When we love someone, we want to be connected to them. The earth "connects" things to itself through gravity. And so, gravity is the attention of the earth.

When we line up our attention with the earth's attention, as in the above exercise, we become connected to the earth and are able to draw on the earth's resources (its energy).

Ideally, spirit breathing is taught individually to each student, according to what is happening in his life.

The spirit breathing cannot call attention to itself as a separate subject because it lies at the root of our existence. The student can only be guided in spirit breathing as an integral part of his life.

There is a fear of joining your attention to the earth's attention. This is because there is always a sneaking suspicion that you will find out something you would rather not know.

Intelligence of the Earth

Intelligence is not something generated by yourself; it is an energy flowing through you from the heaven/earth flow of energy. It is like gravity, something you are aware of and can use.

In another section, the *Gospel* says that to avoid oblivion, one must hear the Father speak his name. In this name are the patterns of our understanding, our world view. It is created or called by the Father and we hear it. Our intelligence flows from our true selves, creativity, which is not individualistic at its deepest level. Rather, we are all emanations of a unified creative force.

The intelligence of each of our cells lies in how it harmonizes with our whole body. The intelligence of each person lies in how we harmonize with the whole earth.

Within our bodies, cellular intelligence is a result of the evolution of communications systems, allowing one cell to respond to what others are doing to maintain the health of the whole.

The same is true on a planetary level. Intelligence is achieved by opening communications not only among people but among all parts of the earth. Intelligence, then, is a matter of connection, and attention is what connects us.

Exercising Attention

Therefore, the next step in spirit breathing is to develop the attention and to connect that attention to other people, animals, and even objects.

Another section of the *Gospel* explains that ". . . the name of the Father is the son," or the Father is formless creativity while the son is formed patterns.

In a Zen story, the student asks the master what is the essence of Zen. The master does not answer and the student takes that as a cue to leave. As the student approaches the door, the master calls out his name and the student immediately turns to face the master. "That's it!" the master explains.

When one of my students asks what attention is, I often clap my hands to make a loud sound and tell the student to notice what took place inside him.

We are so busy noticing the objects of our attention that we don't appreciate attention itself. The next time a loud sound or unusual action captures your attention, notice what is being captured. What does that feel like?

Push Hands helps to build the strength and subtlety of attention. You must respond to the slightest pushes and changes of balance and posture of your partner so that you offer no resistance to his attempts to push you.

There are tiny moments when the alignment of your position, as compared with your partner's, allows you to push your partner off balance. Those moments usually last less than a second. How can you respond quickly enough to, first of all, notice your advantageous position, secondly, push and, thirdly, push at just the correct angle so that your partner can't neutralize your force?

This is done, not through some mechanical technique, but by a "configuration of attention." The force of attention fills your body like air filling a balloon. The advantageous position acts as a pin, bursting the balloon and releasing the force.

This requires connecting your body's movements, breath and attention as described previously. Then, the student divests himself of a single focal point of attention and instead, allows his attention to fill all parts of his body. He has practiced paying attention to each of those parts separately and how the actions of each affect the others. Now his attention (the communication among all these parts) is turned on all at once, and the volume of that attention is turned up and sustained throughout Push Hands. It feels as though it is not the muscles that are holding you up and moving you, but the flow of attention. In this state the muscles can relax and use minimum energy.

Snake Staring

It is difficult to sustain that volume of attention at first. The attention must be exercised to be strengthened. We use "snake staring" to exercise the attention. We perch a Cook's Tree Boa on a branch and stare at it just within its striking range. The Cook's Tree Boas are very high-strung animals. They will even bite at a warm breeze because they are used to eating birds which come in for a landing on a branch. If the bird escapes their bite, the snakes obviously can't follow the birds into the air. So they have a hair-trigger response.

If you stare at them, they will remain still until your attention wavers. Then they bite quickly and they have large teeth. If the student realizes his attention has indeed wavered, he must duck before the snake's mouth reaches his face.

Actually, the students wear goggles for protection. The goggles don't interfere with the staring because the snakes have poor eyesight anyway. They rely on the sense of the energy which flows through the eyes. The student quickly learns to sense this energy and to configure his attention to respond quickly to any alteration in the energy that connects student and snake (just as the snake does naturally). It feels as though the snake's strike is pushing you out of the way. In this way the snake becomes a teacher of attention and is so recognized in many cultures. Snakes are wonderful teachers.

Attention for Sale

Once this configuration of attention is attained, imagery is used to direct the behavior of the force of attention. In the case of Push Hands, the imagery permeates the attention, to trigger the body to push when an advantageous alignment is achieved. The imagery does not have to be visual. Usually it is a feeling, such as a coiled spring or a tiger about to leap.

The force of attention, then, is directed by the feeling of a quality. This idea is very basic in the Madison Avenue advertising world.

Advertisements are not created as much for conveying information as to create the feeling of a quality associated with a product. Television commercials are designed to create a configuration of attention in the viewer so the viewer will be susceptible to being imprinted with the ad. The viewer's attention is the product sold to the advertiser.

The same may be said for religions, political parties, etc. Attention—your attention—is a product which these organizations work to gain. They focus your attention on something meaningless so you think that is the issue, when it is really your attention they want.

You may have been sitting at a fast-food restaurant when your friend pointed out the window and said, "Hey, look at that!" and then proceeded to steal a French fry from your plate. Same idea.

We do that in Push Hands as well. We may come in with force in one area to draw our partner's attention to that area. Then we actually push somewhere else. If you shift the partner's attention more than once a second and continue to do this without stop, his attention will eventually wear out. Then you can do what you want. Such shifting requires only the slightest movement on your part, just a tiny change of hip angle, relaxing or firming a single muscle in the shoulder, etc. This kind of play really builds the network of attention.

Its real benefit is in general health. The easier the parts of the body can communicate, the healthier you will be.

To put it simply, the Form calms the attention. Push Hands teaches the mechanics of attention. The fighting teaches the power of attention.

Fighting requires as much attention as Push Hands but requires faster reaction time. The intimidation factor is also higher.

Centering Attention

You learn a very important lesson in fighting. The attention must emanate from the center (the *tan-tien*). When your attention shifts from one thing to another, it must first return to the center before coming out again. This saves energy, increases your power and your speed, and keeps you centered. It is a strange concept but a very important one in T'ai-chi and one of the most important points to be gained from this book.

Try this exercise. Switch your attention visually between three or four objects. First move the focal point of your attention directly from one object to another.

Next, when you switch your attention, bring the focal point back to your center (tan-tien) first and then to the next object and so on. Your attention will become like one of the children's paddle ball toys (the rubber ball attached to a wood paddle by a long rubber band; the child bounces the ball off the paddle and the rubber band stretches and draws the ball back to the paddle). With the focussing exercise, your punches will become more springy and much faster.

Those whose attention is continually moved from one distraction to another and never bring it back to the center are like those who moved away from their "places . . . when they received error . . ."

Connecting through the Centers

Now the spirit breathers learn to deal with the illusion that we are a single lump of protoplasm plopped into the middle of a universe of colliding objects. When I worked in a youth center, I taught a Zen candle ceremony, "Together Through the Centers." The purpose was to join the participants together in a meditative state.

Push Hands and sparring (free-style fighting) accomplishes the same result. In Push Hands, the relationship of balance between the partners is the focus of each of their attentions. This relationship becomes a living force of its own, a form of life created by the Push Hands partners. When one partner moves or shifts his balance, the other must readjust the relationship through his own movement or shifting of balance.

There are actually three focal points of attention in Push Hands or in any personal interaction. The first is your own center of balance (the tan-tien). The second is your partner's and the third is the relationship between the two. Similarly, within yourself there is a triple focus, on the mind, the body-mind, and the relationship between the two. These two triple focuses can be related to the *I Ching* hexagrams. Christians might also contemplate the meaning of the Holy Trinity in this context.

This triple focus in Push Hands is similar to practicing with the staff (stick) weapon. There are the two ends of the pole and the pivotal point in the center. Yet the pole is obviously one single unit.

Similarly, in Push Hands the two partners feel as if they are a single unit. In fact, they strive to maintain their connectedness. Push Hands is the play of connectedness (following the partner and maintaining balance) and individuality (the push, which creates a separateness).

Yet even when we are pushed we maintain connectedness in the following way. I teach the students to be sensitive to the exact nature of the push. They try, of course, to neutralize the push. But if they are indeed pushed, they allow the pattern of force to be played out. This means that each push comes in with a different pattern of angles of momentum and circular momentums. As the student is pushed, he allows his body to move freely so that his body accurately portrays the pattern of momentums of the push. This may result in getting slammed against the wall and we line the wall with mats for that purpose.

Being slammed into the wall also often results in very pleasurable adjustments to the spine in a chiropractic sense. A student may even offer resistance to the partner so that he is sure to be slammed and adjusted.

And so even within the separateness caused by the push there is a kind of connectedness that is maintained. This is the same kind of connectedness that allows us to feel good about the world around us when things are going poorly. Although we get "pushed" in life, our connection to the earth is so strongly felt that we do not react to our problems by separating ourselves from the rest of the world. In other words, learning replaces anger as the reaction to our troubles. We use each circumstance as a learning experience and trust that much of our problems come from the same type of tension and resistance that gets us in trouble in Push Hands and fighting. We look for an echo of the effects of our own behavior in the circumstances that happen to us.

Sowing Seeds

We may not realize just how much our own actions affect the world around us. In Push Hands, the force of the push mushrooms out. The force seems to continue to grow even after the partners are no longer in contact. This is because of the expansion of internal energy. The push itself is just a seed that grows within the body of your partner. By this process, you learn how you can be aware of creating living energy that has its effects on others.

The exact pattern of the force of the push is something the student is quite aware of. A push can be created with a pattern that can offset any neutralization of the partner (assuming the partner is not as aware and sensitive to these patterns as you are).

When the push first comes out, it is only a seed, a small packet of potential. It grows within the partner in a similar way as the creativity, your true self, sends out a pattern that grows within you. You may choose to play out that pattern (a name), as American Indians do with their vision quest. A vision quester is a seeker of the "name." Or you may try to neutralize it. You may even conflict with it (just as your partner may do with your push) depending on your relationship to creativity (the relationship of the son to the Father). The son is the name of the Father. This means that the pattern of your life issues from your creativity.

Attention Caught in Tangled Webs

The American Indian vision quest is a way of re-discovering the purpose, the thrust of your life. We often become so entangled by everyday matters that our deepest longings are neglected or forgotten. We sacrifice fulfilling these longings in the quest to fulfill needs we are "supposed to have."

In my position as T'ai-chi teacher, I have seen this problem often. At a party, someone may act as if all this is "New Age nonsense" because he thinks this is what he's supposed to believe.

But when he finds out that I'm a T'ai-chi teacher, he will take me on the side and confide his real beliefs. I was at a party where this happened. A man, in his late forties, started telling me about the most far-flung New Age ideas of other planes of existence and all (after finding a place where "we could talk").

It was apparent that his need to talk to other people about his ordinary feelings was stifled. This simple need turned him to studying metaphysical subjects. It would obviously be valuable for him to find people he can communicate with on the level of feeling.

He explained that he didn't dare get involved in "magic" until he cleared up all the inner turmoil he was experiencing. Isn't that silly? What is more magical than clearing up inner turmoil? This fellow needed to let go of the part of himself that felt ashamed at having feelings, so the feelings would be allowed to live. The choice was to possibly lose face or to lose his true life.

"Death" in Push Hands is represented by being pushed—losing. This is why we transform the "losing" by playing out the partner's push, should we fail to neutralize it. The very meaning of losing and winning is changed. Winning means to regain all the parts of yourself and allow them to flourish.

Splattered Attention

The next step in T'ai-chi is kickboxing. You also remain connected to your partner by following every movement. Although you are getting punched and kicked and returning the favor to your partner, the connectedness is the main focus of attention. In fact, your partner tries to break your attention from the connectedness by rapidly altering his pattern of striking, his stance or even his whole style of fighting. If you can become disconnected for even a fraction of a second, he can strike without your being able to respond.

This is not a physical connectedness but a connection of attention. We often say (in an overly melodramatic way) that if your partner splatters your blood with his punches, it isn't as bad as if he splatters your attention. Actually there are very few injuries in our class because the students' bodies are loose and conditioned. But we just love that kind of talk.

Previously, the subject of "the seed" was discussed. The seed is the "name" as it is uttered by the Father. This seed is played out by one's life, by one's behavior. The trick is to fine-tune your attention so that you can hear the name —so that you can make out the patterns of your life, to perceive your deepest needs as a living organism and not have your attention splattered by the events around you.

> For indeed the Father's name is not spoken, but it is apparent through a son. (*The Gospel of Truth*: 47)

> For the name is not from (mere) words, nor does his name consist of appellations, but it is invisible. (Ibid.)

> If he is called, he hears, he answers, and he turns to him who is calling him, and ascends to him. . . . Having knowledge, he does the will of the one who called him, he wishes to be pleasing to him, he receives rest. (Ibid., 40)

This is a nice description of the vision quest.

Alien Seeds

The problem is that many of these seeds do not come from our own creativity. They are programmed into us. The spirit breather must come to know the feeling of his own creativity, the seeds coming from inside himself and then know which patterns of his behavior have been programmed from other sources.

His T'ai-chi practice gives him the knowledge to tell which of these external programmings are beneficial and which are harmful. He can then play Push Hands with the harmful internal programming as he did with his human partner. Using spirit breathing, he dissolves the unwanted programming and its hold over his behavior. As this programming is dissolved, the talons with which it grabbed your behavior are ripped free. It may be an unpleasant experience in some ways but the freedom that is gained more than makes up for the unpleasantness.

> Error was upset, not knowing what to do; it was grieved, in mourning, afflicting itself because it knew nothing. When knowledge drew near it—this is the downfall of (error) and all its emanations—error is empty, having nothing inside. (Ibid., 42)

Notice that *The Gospel of Truth* says that even error has emanations. The unwanted programming does have its effects on our behavior and how we perceive the world around us. When the error, the seeds, the programming, is released, the whole world seems to change.

CHAPTER 5
THE SECRET OF PERSONAL GROWTH

The Father reveals his bosom—now his bosom is the Holy Spirit. He reveals what is hidden of him—what is hidden of him is his Son—so that through the mercies of the Father the aeons may know him and cease laboring in search of the Father, resting there in him, knowing that this is rest. Having filled the deficiency, he abolished the form—the form of it is the world, that in which he served. For the place where there is envy and strife is a deficiency, but the place where (there is) Unity is a perfection. Since the deficiency came into being because the Father was not known, therefore when the Father is known, from that moment on the deficiency will no longer exist. As with the ignorance of a person, when he comes to have knowledge his ignorance vanishes of itself, as the darkness vanishes when light appears, so also the deficiency vanishes in the perfection. So from that moment on the form is not apparent, but it will vanish in the fusion of Unity, for now their works lie scattered. In time Unity will perfect the spaces. It is within Unity that each one will attain himself; within knowledge he will purify himself from multiplicity into Unity, consuming matter within himself like fire, and darkness by light, death by life. (*The Gospel of Truth*: 41)

Now how can we do this? This paragraph makes an important point. How do we know the "real we"? Certainly it takes an unusual experience to realize that we have been acting. Otherwise we would assume that we *are* the way we act and the way we think. Few people have (or admit to having) an experience which challenges this idea.

I was talking with a close friend who had a vague feeling of unfulfillment. It was vague only as to its cause but it was felt very strongly.

I soon understood that she had spent her life trying to be proper and now realized that inner creature, her true self, had not been fulfilled by properness all these years. Yet she was afraid to "be herself" and perhaps lose those close to her.

Certainly many people are not comfortable with change and expect us to act and think in a specific pre-set way all our lives. Growth, however, is like bait on a hook. If you allow the inner creature, the Father, to be in the world, if you live your life from that true self, there will always be others who recognize that and do appreciate you. But you have to fish for them using your real self as bait.

There is a spirit of real selves, a human spirit, a "Holy Spirit" (defined as "his bosom" in this paragraph) which is recognizable.

Another definition in this paragraph, "his Son," is that which you have hidden, those feelings, thoughts and behaviors which are a reflection of the true self. This reminds me of the saying in the New Testament that the stone the builders rejected will become the cornerstone of the new temple.

This Son, which we may understand as a "natural person," a Taoist, lives as an example so that others may know that it is possible to really be oneself. We may then stop searching for that secret mystical world and come to realize that living a simple, natural life is true peace and fulfillment.

Another definition, "the form," is the world as we know it, filled with envy and strife. It is the world view, our understanding of who we are and how everything works.

Yet as much as we may know about this world, there seems to be a deficiency: our own inner peace.

Once we come to rest and allow our true natures to come out, we find that the whole nature of the world changes. It is abolished as we knew it. This is so because the nature of the world as we perceive it depends on the nature of how we perceive ourselves.

Our own self-image has as much to do with the way we see the "outside" world as with any objective facts about the world. When the image is dropped, the world, the form, is abolished.

And then a great secret of Gnostic, Taoist and other training is revealed.

Consuming the Image

Whatever deficiency you may feel you have, this paragraph suggests that its origin can be traced to having fashioned a fake self and believing that it is you. In other words, the entire process of creating an image and believing in it creates the problems in our lives.

Once you drop that image and allow the natural you to express itself, there is no problem anymore.

When you recognize the unity of your experiences, that all you experience is part of you, a wonderful thing happens. "[He consumes] matter within himself, like fire. . . ."

This refers to a startling realization, that is, how much of what we experience is a product of our expectations. Even the solidness of the world and our addiction to that solidness is a result of what we are taught to experience. Through Gnostic, Taoist, etc., training, the way we solidify the world around us and the way we solidify (stiffen) ourselves is consumed as if in a fire and melts away.

This leads to a more relaxed, adaptable way of life and a fluid, growing personality.

Practically, I find that if I keep in mind my true identity and stop complaining about myself and others, this process proceeds automatically.

Simply believing that the world around you is part of yourself and living the implications of that idea leads to much joy and fruitful experience.

The original process of postulating that we are an individual, located here, with certain opinions and behaviors, leads us to a state of mind in which the world appears as a conglomerate of solid objects all knocking into each other —just as we feel we are in a world of ideas knocking into each other.

We thus feel ourselves "knocking into" life at every turn. It is an addictive perspective and has detrimental consequences.

When you listen to the words of *The Gospel of Truth*, allow the inner creature to hear (as this treatise expresses it) words without vowels or consonants, words of truth. Does something within you respond to *The Gospel of Truth*?

Perfecting the Spaces

The beauty of this writing, its directness and poignancy astounds me. For example, on page 41: "So from that moment on the form is not apparent, but it will vanish in the fusion of Unity, for now their works lie scattered. In time Unity will perfect the spaces."

What a great description of Push Hands and T'ai-chi kung-fu. We tend to concentrate on the objects around us and not the spaces between. Each object is viewed in an isolated way. We therefore tend to think of ourselves as an isolated object, one among many.

When we practice Push Hands, the spaces between the arms and bodies take on as much significance as the physical body itself. If we were to concentrate solely on technique, on moving the other person's arms out of the way, we would remain very poor Push Hands players. In Push Hands, we do not counteract the partner's incoming push, but flow around it as water flows around a swimmer's body. In T'ai-chi kickboxing we do not block the opponent but flow around his yang strikes and flow into the yin, unprotected areas. There we deliver our own strikes.

In both Push Hands and kickboxing, I urge the student not to focus his attention on the focal point of the other person's force, but to remove himself from that focal point. The attention should not be on the fist but on the opponent's unprotected yin areas.

When the student is able to accomplish this, ". . . from that moment on the form is not apparent, but it will vanish in the fusion of Unity, for now their [the partner's] works [perceptions] lie scattered." I wish I had said that!

The partner's attention and the forms into which his creativity molded his attention, are broken (lie scattered). They are broken because your own actions were outside of your partner's understanding. You slipped into the spaces between his awareness.

Anyone involved in internal kung-fu will appreciate how your attention can shatter when your partner can slip between the limitations of your attention.

The only way you can slip around like this is to have your attention centered in the tan-tien. Always remain centered. "It is within Unity that each one will attain himself." Only from this center can your attention maintain a balance between form (the solid objects) and emptiness (the spaces). T'ai-chi-Ch'uan practitioners also know that only when the "opponent" becomes a "partner" and the two opposing people seem to join, can true Push Hands or T'ai-chi fighting take place.

When the Push Hands is at its best, the two partners seem to fuse into one being. T'ai-chi also emphasizes unifying (connecting) all the parts within ourselves (physical movement, momentum, breath, attention, etc.).

A Book Is Only a Guide

Practically speaking, it would be difficult to simply read *The Gospel of Truth* and be instantly transformed into a totally fulfilled being. That is why T'ai-chi emphasizes practicing physical exercises with a competent teacher. The philosophy must become concrete in order to really work. The Gnostics used rituals as their physical practice. Their writings served to describe the path underlying their other practices.

Many T'ai-chi teachers have complained that the quality of T'ai-chi has been deteriorating so much that they fear this beautiful practice will soon die out. I feel one of the reasons for this is that many students simply do not understand what they're doing or why. They are told that it is done a certain way because "that's the way my teacher did it and he's the greatest."

This chapter is designed to show that all cultures are really striving for the same things: health, peace of mind, harmony with other people and nature, and eliminating barriers to abilities. By studying what other cultures have to say about these issues and their methods of teaching, we can learn a lot about T'ai-chi and about our own hearts.

CHAPTER 6
WHEN HEALING ERUPTS

If indeed these things have happened to each one of us, then we must see to it above all that the house will be holy and silent for the Unity. (It is) as in the case of some people who moved out of dwellings where there were jars that in spots were not good. They would break them, and the master of the house does not suffer loss. Rather (he) is glad because in place of the bad jars there are full ones which are made perfect. For such is the judgment which has come from above. It has passed judgment on everyone; it is a drawn sword, with two edges, cutting on either side. When the Word came into the midst, the one that is within the heart of those who utter it—it is not a sound alone but it became a body—a great disturbance took place among the jars because some had been emptied, others filled; that is, some had been supplied, others poured out, some had been purified, still others broken up. All the spaces were shaken and disturbed because they had no order nor stability. Error was upset, not knowing what to do; it was grieved, in mourning, afflicting itself because it knew nothing. When knowledge drew near it—this is the downfall of (error) and all its emanations—error is empty, having nothing inside. (*The Gospel of Truth*: 41)

And what if we do accomplish this? "The house" is our own being, our own body. Silence is here described as letting go. First of all, we must let go of the feeling that we need possessions to fulfill ourselves, that we need to own something in order to really be part of it.

This concept creeps into inner development as well. We feel we need to gain "enlightenment" or "secret knowledge." As we look at ourselves, we see deficiencies. In some "spots" you are "not good." The Gnostic teacher doesn't say, "Repair those spots." He tells us to smash the jars and we will suffer no loss. In other words, let go of your ideas of deficiency and your attempts to repair the broken jars. Those deficiencies are not you. They are not deficiencies of the master of the house.

Smash the Deficient Jars

You may be very cautious, for example, when interacting with others lest you do or say something "stupid." It may be hard to believe that your friends like you just for yourself. The solution is not to make doubly sure that you don't do anything stupid. The real solution is to let go of that fear, to really be yourself, to trust yourself and to trust your friends. Trust that you are a good person and they will accept you as you are (as long as you stand up for who you are). Smash the fear of being stupid.

Notice that the *Gospel* mentions that some people are so afraid of having deficiencies that they "moved out of dwellings" (where there were deficiencies). This refers to the way we deny, put down, are ashamed of, dissociate from those parts of us that don't live up to some standard. "Moving out of our dwellings" simply means disconnecting ourselves from ourselves. It means harsh judgements against ourselves just as we harshly judge others.

Simply by your letting go, the master of the house surprisingly finds perfect jars. It reminds me of the saying in both Zen and the New Testament (paraphrased), "If you come to me and say you have a stick, I will give one to you. If you say you do not have a stick, I will take it away from you."

In other words, we also create the forms of our deficiencies. It is not a deficiency of the inner being (master of the house), but of the fashioned creature.

When one of my students is having a problem with a part of his body (say, a tense right shoulder), I suggest that he withdraw his attention from it. This startles him because I usually emphasize filling the whole body with attention.

Yet tension can be caused by too much attention in an area, a blockage to the flow of attention. In such a case, a redistribution of attention is required.

The problem is thus not directly solved, but rather let go of.

I have found that whenever I become embroiled in problems, life solves my problems by giving me an even bigger one. Then I appreciate the comparatively easy time I had before. Life seems to be saying, "Stop complaining or I'll *really* give you something to complain about." This is a kind of redistribution of attention.

Yet when we stop trying to patch up the fashioned creature and allow the master to regain his own house, all is not peaceful.

The inner being, body-mind, is governed by natural law while the fashioned creature is governed by your own made-up rules or those of society. When body-mind regains power you will find that some aspects of your life were in accord with nature (they will be supplied) and others were not (they will be poured out). The stability of your own rules no longer can keep the fashioned creature and its fashioned world together. In other words, your life seems miserable for a time.

My students say that whenever someone says they have read *Movements of Magic*, my students apologize. "We're sorry your life has been ruined."

Yet you realize the emptiness of this make-believe world. When you are faced with the knowledge, the direct experience, of your true nature, this is the downfall of your made-up image.

The Value of Emptiness

Students often complain that the particular punches or pushes I approve of don't feel like anything. That is, when they usually punch they can feel the force and that gives them the feeling that they've done something. But those punches that I say they did well don't give them any feeling of power.

That's because in a proper punch or push, the energy goes cleanly through and is not dissipated on the surface. If the punch's force plays itself out on the skin of your partner, you will feel it, but it will have little effect on the partner. We want the force to enter and resound within the body cavity. It must go cleanly through the skin and muscle layer.

So the image they have of power, in this case feeling the force, interferes with punching well. They must give up this kind of reenforcement, this feeling of being powerful, in order to truly be powerful. The force must cleanly pass through the fist to be effective. In this case the arm feels like a hollow conduit of energy. The bad jars of tensions have been smashed and so the true power can flow through. It is the *space* within the arm (through which the energy flows) that is the value of the arm. Emptiness (yin) thus allows power (yang) to function. In this way, the student "perfects the spaces."

Similarly, students may find that at a certain point in their development, the Form seems to happen by itself without their conscious direction. This shows that their body-minds have taken over.

In such cases, it seems as though imperfect jars (imperfect actions or images) have vanished and in their place are perfect jars. Yet this is disturbing because it does not gratify the mind. It feels like "nothing" because it is efficient.

This is the great difficulty. When the thinking-mind sets itself up as Master, with all its turmoil, at least there's something going on, a lot of action and adventure. When you are efficient, there's not as much melodrama. The loss of melodrama can feel like a death.

Melodrama vs. Simplicity

Yet *The Gospel of Truth* says that it is actually the melodramatic mind that has "nothing inside." This is because true power comes from a deeper, quieter source. Some students come to a T'ai-chi school looking for melodrama—a secret, mysterious teaching, and so forth. And they expect the teacher to be a mysterious, melodramatic person. Then when they see him being human, flaws and all, they are disappointed.

T'ai-chi teaches us simplicity and grounding. While we explore and develop the full potential of human development and experience, our practice is not driven by an unstable mind needing more and more stimulation but by the natural growth of the seed of our being. It is a calm, careful teaching which emphasizes remaining balanced at all stages. Because of this, we can be light-hearted and just "ordinary folks."

I remember one woman asking me why I didn't like to use suntan oil. She thought there was some esoteric reason for it and was surprised when I answered, "Because it's sticky."

And so the *Gospel* talks about a person whose desire to learn comes from a desire to be mystical, so others will be in awe of him. At some point that purpose for learning comes tumbling down.

Laughing at Ineptitude

One of the best learning experiences I had was when I studied with Howard Lee (brother-in-law of Grandmaster William Chen). He came to my school once a week for a few years, after returning from China. My students and I learned several forms of kung-fu from him.

He is an excellent practitioner and a good teacher. Besides the quality of his teaching, the other value of this experience was that my students saw me learning something new right alongside them. They saw me make the same mistakes, and progress as slowly as they did. Howard would do some amazing movement and then ask us to do it. The students and I just looked at each other. We saw that something had happened, but had no idea what.

Several years later I did feel more competent. But while working with Howard Lee, I could actually feel to what degree there was a desire in me to have the students admire my abilities. While it was certainly not a powerful force, it had the potential of controlling my behavior to act in such a way as to be admired rather than to teach in the most effective way possible.

By attending these classes with my students and laughing at our ineptitudes (our "bad jars") I found an even stronger and more realistic bond with the students. I could be human—and flawed—more readily.

The desire to be admired was largely "empty," serving no purpose. But the "bond of ineptitude" was more realistic because it made the classes enjoyable and easier to learn. Competence was obtained without defending the bad jars, the mind's worthless patterns.

Yet how many people are willing to learn for their actual benefit as compared to those who want to learn in order to prop up their self-image? The latter usually are not willing to put in the work, so they drop by the wayside. Very few stick with it. But those who do, become aware of their true selves.

CHAPTER 7
CREATIVITY REGAINS CONTROL

Truth came into the midst; all its emanations knew it. They greeted the Father in truth with a perfect power that joins them with the Father. For everyone loves the truth because the truth is the mouth of the Father; his tongue is the Holy Spirit. He who is joined to the truth is joined to the Father's mouth by his tongue, whenever he is to receive the Holy Spirit. This is the manifestation of the Father and his revelation to his aeons: he manifested what was hidden of him; he explained it. For who contains if not the Father alone? All the spaces are his emanations. They have known that they came forth from him like children who are from a grown man. They knew that they had not yet received form nor yet received a name, each one of which the Father begets. Then when they receive form by his knowledge, though truly within him, they do not know him. But the Father is perfect, knowing every space within him. If he wishes, he manifests whomever he wishes by giving him form and giving him a name, and he gives a name to him and brings it about that those come into existence who before they come into existence are ignorant of him who fashioned them. (*The Gospel of Truth*: 42)

What is it like to live with this awareness? An earlier paragraph refers to a "Word" which is not a sound alone. It is within the heart of those who utter it. It became a body. This word has the power to overthrow the fake kingdom of the fashioned creature and its emanations or forms.

Truth came into the midst. When the fashioned image is speaking, of course, this is not the truth. A person tied to his self-image says things to reinforce that image in the minds of others. His speaking is designed to cause an effect on the hearer. Very often, he will limit his speaking to a further definition of his created identity. "I like this. I believe that. What I would do would be . . . ," etc.

And two such images engage in maintaining the seeming reality of their existence. Truth though, is the mouth of the Father. "Truth" means simply responding truthfully to what is asked—to reveal truth in the most simple meaning of that term. It is straightforward talk, not to cause effect but to convey information. Search your own soul to discover what manner of speaking you engage in.

Yet how would you know if it is your inner being speaking?

"He who is joined to the truth is joined to the Father's mouth by his tongue, whenever he is to receive the Holy Spirit."

Spontaneity

Or, as my students would say, "How is it that whenever you say I'm doing something correctly, it doesn't feel as if I'm doing anything?" This means living spontaneously. When beginning students are about to punch, they go into some big routine first, hunching their shoulders, scowling, etc. We say they are "telegraphing" their intentions. This telegraphing not only tips off the partner but also interferes with your punch. When you punch spontaneously, there is no telegraphing. Spontaneity means being joined to the Father or to the Father's mouth.

The inner creature is the one who actually created the fashioned creature. It is creativity, the Father of the son. Creativity is the yang energy—it fashions. Attention is the yin energy—it receives impressions. Creativity is the forming. Attention is the substance. Mind is the inertia, holding the form in place.

When the Father (your true self) is using your tongue, then your true spirit comes out.

Early in my T'ai-chi teaching I would feel a great urge to say something but since I couldn't think of what I wanted to say, I resisted the urge. Then I started giving in to that urge.

This is what happens. I call the students together and tell them there is something I want to say to them. Yet I have no idea what that might be. One part of me is saying (to myself), "You idiot. Now everyone is looking at you and you don't have anything to say. Now you're in trouble."

Yet, words do emanate from my mouth and as I listen to myself, I must admit that I had something valuable to say. It may even be something I've never thought of before.

When putting on my "The Animal Man" programs (described later in this book) I often bring a new animal into the act. I purposely do not prepare what I will say about it. As I take it out of the box and present it to the audience, I must first come up with something to say about it and then present it in a way that ties in with the rest of the program.

This helps keep me on my toes but more importantly, forces me to rely on that inner being.

I "allow" body-mind to speak. Yet the "I" which is making this allowance is a creation of body-mind itself.

The Creator and the Created

In the middle of writing a science fantasy novel, at one point the characters started talking back to me. This is actually a common occurrence for novelists. In this case, I wanted the story to go one way but the characters had other ideas. Finally one of the characters admonished me. "You are only a translator of our experiences. You have nothing to say about how this story goes!" I had to reach an internal compromise between allowing the characters their own free will and maintaining control over the story. The characters can be considered the emanations while I, in this case, was the Father of those characters.

Isn't this what happens in our lives? We fashion our personalities so we can be powerful in the world and have influence over others. But then the personality takes over and becomes somewhat independent of the one who created it. A compromise has to be reached between your actual self and the patterns of the personality you created. The problem arises when you forget that the personality was created and identify solely with the personality. Your true self then seems like an enemy of the personality. Since we cannot conceive of our enemy as residing within ourselves, we project the feeling of an enemy on other people, countries, ideologies, and so forth.

Of course, there is no enemy. The problem is just that we forgot that this being we identify with was created by our true selves. That is the basic premise of *The Gospel of Truth* and any discipline of self-realization.

You once dreamed of who you would like to become and spent your life working to become that dream. "When a dream becomes flesh trouble is not far behind," unless you know it is a dream. That is why disciplines such as Zen and Buddhism say that people live in a dream. Your dream person can be a humble, spiritual being as well. The dream image can come in any shape, form and color. Living in the "proper" dream is no help to you and that is why I find it difficult to be at "consciousness centers" (places where "enlightened" people get together).

I once went to a meeting of fifteen or so such people. They had called together all the "spiritual" teachers on Long Island for a special purpose. Here, they said, sit the most enlightened people on Long Island and we are going to make the entire world enlightened by the year 2000. That was their goal.

I asked how we were going to do this. The leader responded that we were going to teach people how to let go of their egos. I asked, "How could you do that when you have the biggest egos of all? You think you're better than everyone else."

I was never invited back to that group.

I guess the characters in my story were saying the same thing to me. Perhaps in that case, my thinking-mind and body-mind were using the novel to compete for power. Writing is probably the closest I come to having a religion as it is such a wonderful channel for the writer's growth.

Will the Real Author Please Stand Up

The writers of old often claimed that their books were really written by Lao-tsu or Chuang-tsu or some other famous person. This was because it was considered presumptuous for an ordinary person to write books of wisdom. This has caused considerable trouble among historians trying to separate the true writings of such historical figures from the "phonies."

Of course being "phonies" didn't make their writings any less valuable. In the phenomenon of mediumship, a person speaks the words of a spirit whose body has died. Far be it from me to question the reality of mediumship. But I suspect at least some people become mediums because of the discomfort of simply giving advice under his or her own name. After all, who would pay attention to Joe or Jane Shmoe? People would rather hear Beethoven or King Tut speaking through Jane Shmoe.

Whatever one calls this process, in each case a part of the person must step aside and allow something else to pass through. This involves a trust that whatever passes through is valuable. There is also a recognition involved. When that information, that "Word" wants to come through, I recognize it and defer to it. I, as an emanation, as a creation, know the boss when he shows up. Or as *The Gospel of Truth* says, the emanations ". . . greeted the Father in truth with a perfect power that joins them with the Father."

Inner Voice

When I was four years old, I realized that I didn't really understand what the world was about. (How could I at four, the thought comes to me now!) I knew that I must find teachers or teachings to guide me. At that time, a voice came to me and did, indeed, guide me, and did so very well. This voice was obviously none other than myself.

When I was around twenty-one and had spent my life studying and practicing various disciplines, I came to a point where I wanted to throw away "all this nonsense" and just live like everyone else. I chased that voice away and hoped it would never return.

A couple of months later, I realized what I had lost and tried to get that voice back. It didn't come back as a voice but rather as part of myself (many years later). It was integrated.

Since then I learned that this is a natural process in the ancient systems of training I was exposed to. In order to integrate the parts of yourself into one whole, the student often leaves the teacher or the teachings and considers his training to have been a waste of time. But then, when time has allowed the training to work its magic and transform the student, the student's tongue becomes joined to the creative force which is his true nature. His will comes equally under the control of mind and body-mind. And the mind easily defers to body-mind whenever the creative spirit needs to pass through.

The Rusty Hinges of Life

This passing through is often called "the gate" and the ability to allow movement in and out of the gate is called "the gatekeeper." There are many stories in all cultures about gates and gatekeepers. Can you find the gatekeeper within yourself? A gate that is kept shut is a blockage. The T'ai-chi student must oil the hinges on his gates from time to time.

"For who contains if not the Father alone? All the spaces are his emanations . . . ." All that we know is but a product of our true nature—creativity. The joy and the sorrow. The ineptitude and the skill.

I remember that when I was a child it seemed difficult to hear people and I kept saying, "What?" to get them to repeat what they said. It turned out that I had no hearing problem, but my father was an immigrant and he had trouble understanding people because he wasn't used to the "accent." He had to ask people to repeat themselves and I started imitating him. Also I realized that I didn't really pay attention to what other people were saying because I was paying too much attention to what I was thinking. When I realized all this, I found it easy to hear what other people were saying. I realized that the sounds were, indeed, coming into my ear and brain and I needed to rearrange my method of perception rather than to have people repeat themselves.

I say this because our lives are filled with little things like this. These are the rusty hinges of our lives. If we can look inward and examine the mechanics of our attention we can once again become the artists of our own lives.

See Yourself

Once we understand this, we understand that much of what we want in life is within our grasp.

The first step is to really watch ourselves and thus to see ourselves. I call this step "see yourself." When you chew food, notice the skill of your mouth and tongue. Try this without interfering with that skill, as a passive observer. Allow the mouth and tongue their freedom, their intelligence in the skills they know best. Watch them as you would watch television.

Notice other body skills in the same way—breathing, stretching, yawning, etc., again without interfering.

Notice how your mind works, how one thought follows another. (That was my Zen koan at age eleven or twelve and it astonished me.) Notice where your attention goes. But allow the mind and the attention their freedom. Don't interfere.

Notice how you interact with another person, how your feelings are continually changing as you interact, how you choose words to express your feelings.

Notice the changes of expression on your face. Look at yourself in a mirror and allow your expression to change *without interference*.

Be Yourself

This lack of interference I call "being yourself."

"See yourself. Be yourself." Awareness without interference. Work with another person. Stare into each other's eyes and allow your expressions to fluctuate, even into laughter. But keep your eyes fixed on each other.

When practicing the Form, notice how each little muscle works (or doesn't, as the case may be). When making a decision, notice what criteria, what issues, you use to decide.

Appreciate Yourself

Then "appreciate yourself." Appreciate your complexity, all the things you've learned. Appreciate the emanations.

"See yourself. Be yourself. Appreciate yourself." Try this exercise: Don't put yourself down and don't be angry at yourself, for a full month. See what changes that puts you through. Anger is an emanation of the mind. It is not a direct emanation from creativity but one coming from the fashioned creature.

An example of an emanation of creativity is the T'ai-chi Form. An example of an emanation of the fashioned creature is clenching your teeth when you realize you've made a mistake.

The realization of the mistake *without* the clenching of the teeth is true self-awareness. The clenching of the teeth is self-consciousness. It is your concern about the effect of that mistake on your self-image.

When the clenching of the teeth is dropped, you appreciate yourself. "They greeted the Father in truth with a perfect power that joins them with the Father." You are joined to yourself in true awareness. You can then experience the joy of life.

CHAPTER 8
BURIED TREASURES OF KNOWLEDGE

If I have had any hesitation in commenting on *The Gospel of Truth* as an example of encoded texts it is because it seems self-explanatory. I feel a bit foolish explaining what has been written in a straightforward manner. Yet some of my students say that while they concur with my explanations, they could not have understood a paragraph of this treatise on their own.

This is astounding to me. If *The Gospel of Truth* is encoded, it is only because we scramble the information in our brains. How clearly does one have to write to be understood?

Did you, when reading these paragraphs, understand them in a different way? Were they clear to you from the start? I would love to find out.

Perhaps you can go looking for other sources of knowledge, hidden sources. Realize that they are hidden only by our own ignorance. I would suggest watching the children's video "The Last Unicorn," which we use as a teaching tool at the school. There are many "buried treasures" waiting for discovery.

Another student of William Chen once told me that he believed Master Chen withholds some of his teachings, and those he has never taught anyone. That seemed unbelievable, knowing how hard Master Chen works to teach his students and how he keeps inventing new ways to convey his knowledge.

When I studied with him years ago, he would ask us, even beg us, to ask him questions. Very few people ever did. But I made sure to have a question or two for him during each lesson. This required that I pay close attention to what he was teaching so I could think of questions. Master Chen was very happy to answer each question. I also noticed that few students ever watched him do the Form during class. The students were in their own world. In this way, they were wasting valuable chances to learn. In my own school, I'm only too glad to teach whatever I may know. The idea that knowledge is being withheld for some egotistical reason or any other reason seems ludicrous.

Just look around you, ask questions and put in the effort to practice what you learn, and you will find the living book of the living and perhaps even your own self.

It should be obvious that neither *The Gospel of Truth* nor my own books are designed to be read at one sitting. The words are chosen to stimulate the reader's thoughts, to stir recollections of feelings and to challenge preconceived ideas.

You may prefer to read a paragraph and then put the book down for awhile to let your thoughts and feelings wander.

After reading *Movements of Magic* or *Movements of Power* through once, you may wish to open it to a random page and pick any paragraph.

These are really workbooks, which you can use throughout your life. My students tell me that each time they read Volume I they understand it better or perhaps just differently.

I try to write in a living way so that my words are directed to the body-mind. When your body-mind recognizes something you are reading, it will stir and you will notice it stirring. In this way, I hope to call your body-mind by "name" many times until you recognize it.

Rather than listing "facts" about T'ai-chi or repeating what others have said, I want to have T'ai-chi come alive within the reader. This is a difficult task and I don't know if I have the talent to fully accomplish it, but I feel the need to try. That is my own "name," my seed, my vision. And while I would hate to have someone say, "You did a lousy job," I cannot let that fear stop me from allowing my seed to grow. Perhaps, by daring to share my vision, others may gain the courage to share theirs.

Otherwise, we will be doomed to repeating stories of the visions of others. Our own spirits will die and along with them, the spirit of T'ai-chi-Ch'uan. That is why this volume is dedicated to the *power* of T'ai-chi-Ch'uan, the power of creativity, which each of us can unleash to preserve the human spirit.

CHAPTER 9
LIVING MYTHOLOGICALLY

One problem I have with mythology or philosophical writings is that they can veer very far from one's practical everyday life. How can the principles of mythology, for example, actually help us live our lives?

Here is an example, one which is personal and lies at the core of my own life. When I was four years old, I felt that I needed to find teachers or teachings other than those of my parents (who had trained me in inner awareness and nature awareness since birth). I felt that it was easy to make things up and that unless you are really aware of what you know for real, as opposed to what you think to be true, you could wind up in a web of your own imagination. It would be hard to escape from such a web.

Since I was only four, I felt it would be worth the effort to keep track of the validity of my knowledge because that effort would serve me all my life.

At twelve years old, I still had not discovered what I believed to be a coherent teaching that incorporated science as well as one's inner dynamics. So I felt somewhat powerless in my quest to understand other people and the way our society works, except on a political and economic level. My parents had encouraged me to read the *New York Times* every day, beginning at age eight (but did not encourage me to play ball and engage in sports, unfortunately), so I understood economics and politics.

I also spent much of my time working with animals because I could understand them (as opposed to people) and actually started an animal importing company when I was fourteen.

Vow to the Earth

I made a vow at that time, a vow to the earth, that if I ever did understand the world around me and really got a handle on my life, that I would spend my life teaching that to others. At that time, the furthest I could comprehend my life was to age forty. I vowed to live as if I would die at forty, teaching as much as I could.

Since I felt a total connection to the earth, my vow to the earth felt truly binding.

I did, in fact, learn a great deal and spent my working life teaching, including my "The Animal Man" programs, T'ai-chi, and shamanistic healing.

When I reached thirty-nine (this year) I realized that if I continued to work as hard as I had been, I might indeed die at forty. To survive, I needed to quit "The Animal Man" shows because of their intensive time demands and travel schedules.

The teachings I have been exposed to during my life have emphasized living your life mythologically and connecting the outer events of your life to inner decisions about how you live. And given my original vow at age twelve, I felt that I needed an actual event in my life to help me decide whether to quit "The Animal Man" shows. This event would have to be in the nature of a death/re-birth experience because I had vowed to live my life as if I were going to die at forty. I knew that such mental programming could actually cause an effect on the body. If I expected to die at forty, this in itself might cause poor health at forty, if not death. The mind's expectations are powerful. That is why it would not have been enough just to say, "Okay, I'm forty now and so I'll change my life."

So the death/re-birth experience had to be convincing, not just some ritual I made up. Right around my thirty-ninth birthday I received a letter from a woman I had gone out with two years before, informing me that she had AIDS and that I had better be tested. It turned out that I am healthy—I don't have AIDS. But before the test results came through, I thought I was a goner.

My body immediately began to weaken and I realized this was a case of voodoo medicine—tell someone they may have a deadly disease and the shock alone will injure the body, perhaps to the point of death.

I immediately began thinking about folk remedies I'd heard of, and kept in mind that I had to remain calm and that the results might come out in my favor, anyway.

Vow Renewed

One day, I stood out in my backyard and the lushness of the trees, the beauty of the multicolored flower blossoms, the warm sun and cool spring breeze affected me deeply. I thought that I surely didn't want to leave this beauty prematurely.

I tuned into the earth (through Earth Initiation methods we use at the T'ai-chi-Ch'uan school) and asked, what can I sacrifice to be assured of not having AIDS? Of course, I knew that I either had it or didn't have it. But I try to live my life mythologically and this was an appropriate thing to do within a mythological context.

I immediately realized that I had to sacrifice "The Animal Man" shows if for no other reason than to get reasonable amounts of sleep and keep my immune system strong. I vowed to do so in "exchange" for being healthy. After making that vow, I realized that it was as strong a vow as my original vow at age twelve. It was not a vow I could go back on, whatever the financial consequences.

That vow linked my thirty-nine-year-old self to my twelve-year-old self and closed a circuit in my life, creating a completion. It released me to enter the next stage of my life.

In anthropology there is a concept called "sacred time," as opposed to "profane time." Sacred time means living your life in a mythological context. Profane time is ordinary clock time. Many tribal cultures revere sacred time (hence the name) and find that adhering to one's myth, one's vision, creates a whole different experience of life.

For this reason, they will choose (or be given) a special name that represents their vision. In my own case, the experience that united my twelve-year-old self with my thirty-nine-year-old self shifted my attention to the underlying story of my life. It shifted me back to sacred time.

This helped me to see myself, not as an individual groping and fighting for a share of life's pie, but as part of the web of life, as part of the greater creativity, working for its benefit. We need that shift of attention at times.

Obviously, I would have preferred not to receive that letter, both for the woman's sake and for my shock in receiving it. But it is often said that you should be careful about what you ask for (in this case, a death/re-birth experience) because you might get it.

Further tests on the woman showed no sign of AIDS. It may have been a false positive. Of course, if my tests had come back positive, I would probably have been singing a different tune. Even so, the inner direction of your life can keep you steady through adversity.

Letting Go to Grow

Another part of my vow at age thirty-nine was that whatever good I'd done in the world, whatever "good" credit I had, I would cash in all my chips to stay healthy. This helped to move me into another stage of life as well.

There is a tendency for me to sacrifice my own life—times just spent enjoying life, in order to "do good things." This second part of the vow is helping me to let go of feeling good about myself only when helping others. It is allowing me to spend more time on my own health and fun.

As in "The Boy and the Eagle" story, I wanted to sacrifice my health by working so hard, just as the boy wanted to kill the eagle. A gust of wind (worrying if I had AIDS) brought me face-to-face with the prospect of death, and that allowed me to let go of the behavior that was injuring my spirit (working so hard). The unity of the spirit and the practical side of my life was then realized, and allowed a better balance between the two.

I had been very good at putting off this necessary rebalancing. In *Movements of Magic*, I discussed how this had led to an injured neck, as if the body were saying, "You keep this up and I'll force you to slow down."

While I did slow down somewhat, I can imagine that life itself said, "If a sprained neck won't get you to slow down more, how about AIDS?" Apparently that was enough to convince me. I can be thickheaded at times.

A mythological life is a life of learning. There is little room for complaining because each event is an opportunity to understand yourself better. Your vision is your guide and life is your teacher. And when you do die, the only account that will matter will be not the one in the bank but the one in the hearts of those you helped and those who shared love with you.

There are greater deaths than when your body rots into the earth and provides food for new plants and animals. That kind of death is only a change of shape, not a change of consciousness.

As my parents put it when I was little, "You only die when you stop learning."

SECTION II

The Dynamics of Attention

CHAPTER 10
ATTENTION!

Just as there are physical dynamics in T'ai-chi-Ch'uan to be learned, there are dynamics of the attention. Attention is experienced as a force, much like gravity or momentum, which has specific properties. This force is channeled by a T'ai-chi-Ch'uan student, like the force of a Push Hands partner is channeled through the body, to be neutralized or returned to the partner.

Note that this perspective of attention is quite different from that of considering attention to be something we "own" and then "place" onto various objects, as in "I" put "my" attention "onto" my hands.

The student not only channels physical force in a neutral, non-forceful fashion, but does the same with attention. You know that you are in this state when the body-mind takes over, the Form proceeds organically and you have no idea how you were able to complete the Form.

Two Modes of Attention

This is similar to realizing, after driving for awhile, that you had not been "paying attention to" driving and yet, somehow, you were able to drive efficiently. There are thus two modes of attention or two states of being, differentiated by the relationship between attention and the mind, will and body. In one state the attention locks onto parts of our experience and jumps from one thing to another in a jerky manner. Such a state of being is easily discernible in one's Form, as the Form will not be smooth. It is also discernible in Push Hands as there will be little sensitivity or "listening." The person in such a state will just push and shove and try at all costs to "win." When the attention is locked up by the thinking mind, it turns into the "shape" of the mind—rigid, chaotic and easily distracted.

But when attention is distributed throughout the body-mind (the "intelligence," the sensitivity of each organ, cell and molecule), the attention turns into that "shape," a balanced, ecological system. The Form is smooth and flowing. The Push Hands is sensitive and connected.

Thus attention is, indeed, a force much like momentum which also takes on the "shape" or characteristic of either the thinking-mind or body-mind. The momentum will be jerky if the Form is controlled by the thinking-mind and it will be smooth and flowing if controlled by body-mind. The very quality of your life will be similarly affected.

Individuality

There is a great fear here. If attention is a force flowing through you, then what of your individuality—the "I win, you lose" feeling? Creativity is also experienced as a force flowing through you and likewise, even "will" is not experienced as an isolated, individualistic, "I win, you lose" type of thing.

Whether in Push Hands or free fighting, the two partners merge in terms of will, momentum and creativity. It is a pleasure for a teacher to see a student who spent a number of years in a hard-style school, gradually give up his or her fear, anger and desperation and allow free fighting to become a joyful, albeit full-force, no-rules, playful game.

When he can receive a full-force blow to the head and feel no anger (nor pain because he neutralizes the force internally), he has taken a step toward that second state of being.

The play of Push Hands, fighting or even the Form, then becomes a method of exercising the attention, of learning to channel attention.

The student is then faced with a veritable community of beings—the creativity being, the attention being, the emotion being, the thinking being, the being of will, etc. These are all experienced as forces flowing through him, or creatures interacting with each other in an ecological inner community.

He becomes the center of harmony of those beings—the balancing force. The quality of the student's Form, Push Hands and fighting is an expression of this balance and harmony.

When two such students spar together, the resultant quality of the sparring is an expression of the balance and harmony of those two communities of beings. This is the "shamanistic," the "alchemical" aspect of T'ai-chi-Ch'uan, an aspect sorely missing in modern times.

It is a method of rejuvenation based on understanding all the "elements" of a human being and how to keep them in balance so that life will be joyful.

As an example of how learning the dynamics of attention is essential to this process, let's take one aspect of the Form. The momentum of an arm would interact with the momentum of the torso and a leg.

The student learns to connect the focal point of his attention to the crest of the wave of momentum so that both are flowing smoothly together. Since there are actually several such flows of momentum and several such crests, the student learns to divide the attention so that several "flows" of attention are connected to several flows of momentum.

In the case above, one focal point of attention would flow along with the crest of the wave of momentum of the arm, another with the torso and a third with the leg.

Imagine the difficulty of being aware of several things going on at once in the body and perceiving the intricate interactions among the various momentums. This is greater awareness than we are usually used to.

This process is crucial in "Chi-gung," an advanced T'ai-chi-Ch'uan practice. Since attention is not an "object" owned by the student, but rather a universal force, the above process is possible. If attention were like an object, it could only be at one place at a time. But it is more like momentum or gravity which is everywhere at once.

Furthermore, as the flows of momentum interact and influence each other, so do the flows of attention. As the student progresses, he can divide the attention into finer and finer flows, corresponding to finer flows of momentum, until the whole body becomes enlivened with attention.

The obvious question is, "What part of the student is doing all this learning if the student is a community of beings?" In other words, who is in control inside us?

Words, of course, can only serve to describe the experience. In fact, in all my writings, I try to describe my own experiences rather than to repeat dogma, as I find I can speak honestly only of what I have experienced.

But consider nature. How do the plants and animals grow? How does evolution take place? We could analyze these questions biochemically or zoologically, but to generalize, this is the "way of nature."

And T'ai-chi-Ch'uan teaches us to live naturally. This means to experience the forces and dynamics of nature and to live in harmony with those dynamics.

There is no single "part" of the student controlling all the other parts. The student is taught about balance, letting go of blocks to the attention so that attention is distributed evenly throughout the body.

This is "the way of the body," the natural way our being is designed to work. The student does not have to make himself work this way, but merely removes obstacles to his natural functioning.

When the obstacles are removed, attention illuminates the natural dynamics like a searchlight, revealing internal surroundings. Then the student knows exactly what to do.

The Flow of Attention

Getting back to the flow of momentum in the Form, attention can flow out of our body in the same way momentum does. Obviously, the momentum created when we do the Form is not restricted to within the body. Momentum may flow out the legs, palms, or even, inappropriately, the shoulders.

As we stop turning in one direction and start turning in another, the momentum (and attention) may flow through a leg, into the earth and circle around back to move in the other direction. This movement beneath the earth is part of what is called "the root."

Even though the movement seems to double back on itself, or perhaps move at a right angle, the movement is really smooth and circular, because the momentum and attention is smooth and circular, circling around beneath the feet.

When two T'ai-chi-Ch'uan partners are fighting, their attentions connect and interpenetrate their bodies so that they are aware of the intentions (the movements of attention) of the partner. They even try to use that awareness in making fake movements (or even fake internal intentions) to confuse the partner. They will strike only when they feel the partner's attention is unable to respond, and, in fact, try to manipulate the partner's attention so he is unable to respond. This is called "freezing the partner's attention."

The ability to channel attention, then, is a central issue in T'ai-chi-Ch'uan. I would say that if the dynamics of attention are not being taught, then T'ai-chi-Ch'uan is not being taught.

Attention is the yin force; it is the very substance of the universe. Creativity is the yang force; it is the shaping of that substance. The student's movements are controlled by the interaction of yin (attention) and yang (creativity) and not by thinking, "Let's see, what move comes next?"

Lovemaking is an excellent example to use for feeling the state of an accomplished student. When you are making love, there are two wills blending with each other. There is a play of the surrender of your will to the other with the exercising of your will.

The same is true in the T'ai-chi student. Only when the will of the thinking-mind surrenders and the will of creativity is allowed to interact directly with attention, can the student truly experience the internal aspect of T'ai-chi-Ch'uan.

Many people repeat the movements over and over for years and learn all sorts of clever Push Hands techniques, yet they still feel something lacking in their T'ai-chi practice.

Becoming Aware of Attention

The first step out of this dilemma is to be aware of the force of attention—to pay attention to attention. This doesn't mean thinking. It means that whenever your attention is distracted, notice that which is being distracted. Don't worry about what is distracting you (unless it is a big truck headed your way).

Use every opportunity of being distracted to come to know attention. Again this doesn't mean knowing something about it. Attention is the very substance of life. When you get to know the substance, you will know (you will feel) how creativity shapes it.

Notice how the flow of momentum through the Form affects attention. Root the attention (let it sink through the feet) and notice how that affects the momentum. "Pay" attention only to the momentum and notice how that affects the physical movements of the body.

When you begin to identify yourself more with attention, momentum and creativity than with thoughts, then your will shifts from the thinking-mind to the body-mind. Your will becomes the messenger of nature, organizing your behavior.

It is as if you came to live among a group of animals. You would get to know them as individuals and would come to identify yourself as part of their community. Your behavior toward them would begin to reflect their natures because they would only understand you within the context of their animal culture.

The same is true of the natural parts of yourself. As you come to identify with attention and creativity, your behavior will adapt to the "culture," the dynamics of those forces.

And those dynamics are biological. Attention is composed of all the awareness, all the sensitivities of the organs, cells and molecules of our bodies. It contains the power, the "wisdom" of trillions of little awarenesses. Through the process of evolution, one-celled animals gradually formed into communities to eventually form multicellular animals such as ourselves.

For the multicellular community to function, a vast array of communication networks had to develop so the whole system could be coordinated and kept in balance. Within the awareness of our internal parts lies a billion years of evolutionary experimentation with the principle of balance.

The T'ai-chi student allows his attention to function in its original biological state and is thus reunited with his evolutionary heritage. This is called "returning home" in Zen Buddhism.

Attention will come to have an inertia—a tendency to remain in its biological state—and will not be distracted easily. The body of such a person will seem more alive than the average person. It will seem to possess the agility and sensitivity of an animal because we are, indeed, natural animals under our manufactured clothes and our manufactured mind.

In my opinion, T'ai-chi is the teaching of attention and all the exercises are designed to enhance the original super-intricate communications system that evolved over billions of years.

If we can become aware of the dynamics of attention, we will have an insight into the mechanism of nature herself.

CHAPTER 11
THE HEALING FORCE

As you send your energy out from your body, you can tell that there is another living "being" just at and beyond the surface of your skin which then takes the energy and uses it. Thus you understand that all is alive; living beings occupy all space. You also understand that attention is not owned by you; it is the lifeblood of the earth that flows through you and is used by all creatures, as blood nourishes all the cells of the body.

Letting go of attention is part of love. In connecting two people together, it is the attention that connects. This energy must flow between you. Yet if you identify attention as yourself, you may be afraid to let it go because it seems to be part of you.

But really, it is your connections that are your power. It is the connections that are love and so you need not fear losing your identity. Love shows you your true identity. Your identity is not the holding back of attention but that channeling of attention that the artist works with—creativity.

When you scorn, when you hate, you break the flow. When you laugh, when you love, you reconnect that flow.

The creature at your boundary is body-mind. Body-mind is life itself. Your attention can flow through all the levels of body-mind, even the planetary level. It can focus down to the tiniest levels, such as the cells. The teaching of the dynamics of attention develops this ability. It allows you to release your attention to flow in any direction. At the same time, it teaches you that the attention must still remain centered in the tan-tien so you will remain grounded and (very importantly) so the nutrients (lessons, observations) absorbed by the attention can flow back to benefit you as an individual.

Relationships

When you allow "your" attention to flow out and mingle with other energies, the individualistic feeling can get lost. This is a problem for some people in relationships. Some people feel that they "lose themselves" in a relationship. That is why it is important to keep attention centered and grounded while it is allowed to flow outward. The result is a sort of stretching. These pathways of attention can allow the student to feel the inner state of his teacher and learn much more than just the outer movements of T'ai-chi-Ch'uan.

Imagine a student who only learns by imitating his teacher. This student doesn't internalize his teacher's lessons but rather, becomes a clone. He has allowed his attention to be disconnected from his center and has allowed his teacher's behavior patterns to replace his own. He is thus just acting. He will always have a gnawing feeling that something is wrong.

Another student may not allow his attention to flow to the teacher. So he only picks up the surface level of what his teacher is showing and not the spirit. He hasn't really changed on the inside. In the perfect balance, the student does change, but along his own path of development, not his teacher's.

Your greatest teacher, the creature at the boundary of your skin, is just waiting there, ready to teach you whatever you want to know and things you've never even dreamed of.

Yet there are other forces waiting there too, ready to trap your attention—advertisers, religions and other forces on an energy level. T'ai-chi-Ch'uan teaches you to recognize the natural creature and avoid getting trapped by other forces. It allows you to remain grounded while your attention is free to travel.

Animating the Body

The movement of the pulse of attention (the attention that flows out of your body) through the levels of body-mind, I call the "spiral staircase." It also may be likened to an elevator moving through the different floors of a building.

To put it very simply, the individual human body is but one level on which you exist. It is a point you can focus on. The interplay of attention and creativity can move to other physical objects and to other kinds of experiences. The animating of a human body is a creative act that we are involved in at every moment. This animating is affected by how we creatively use attention.

When we see a person move and talk, we assume that he is alive. This may be so on a biological level, but on another level there are many "walking dead" among us. I have encountered or heard or read about many relationships in which someone considered their partner to be "alive" or animated. Yet after awhile they realized that the partner was not fully relating to them as a human being.

This "unanimated" partner's behavior consisted of a complex series of programmed behaviors. When feelings were brought up for discussion, the partner simply did not respond. Such a discussion was outside of the partner's awareness. Soon, it became obvious that there was really no relationship going on, even though the two people may have been married.

If awareness is bound up in programmed behavior, anything outside the program is treated as if it did not exist. When people get involved in a relationship, they assume their partner is aware of the world around and within them. The "unanimated" person assumes that everyone works on the basis of programmed behavior. So when there is a mixed relationship, there is much confusion. Each person tries to convert the other. The difference is that an aware person channels attention creatively and wants to interact with others on that basis.

This section, and indeed the whole book, is really a discussion of how we animate our own bodies and the mechanics of that process. It is something we can directly feel, and the words simply point out what is already going on inside you. I suggest that we all have a responsibility to gain skill in this process, to be as effective in our lives as possible.

This skill doesn't require any gadgets or electronic devices. It only needs an honest attempt to study and to focus your attention inward to see what is going on inside.

Seeing Inside Yourself

As you "travel" in this way, you begin to see the connections between the levels. For example, you can experience how your social interactions affect the tension patterns in your musculature. You can experience how your endocrine glands are affected by watching an exciting television show. These are obvious and simple examples.

Yet there are people who become emotionally upset when their physical body has problems. They are unaware that the chocolate sundae they just ate is throwing their body mechanisms off because of the intense dose of sugar. They may go through their lives thinking they are unhappy about their circumstances when these unhappy feelings are actually coming from their assaults against their own body.

I call this "linkage," which means knowing the source of your feeling. Our behaviors are linked to our feelings. If we feel bad, we may be irritable. If we "link" this bad feeling to some outside circumstance, let's say someone you don't like the looks of, you may punch him in the nose as a result of your bad feeling. But if you recognize the bad feeling as coming from the chocolate cake, your response may be to refrain from eating more cake. If the person over there is a lot bigger and stronger than you, such a mistake in linkage could have serious consequences.

In a similar way, there are types of energy that can affect us on other than the chemical level (in this example the chemical is the dose of sugar). The change in the earth's flow of energy when the seasons change is an example. To be able to detect such changes in energy, your own attention must be very smooth and fluid.

Internal Pathways of Attention

When students first learn to expand their attention on the in-breath (while doing the Form), they may find lumps in this smooth expansion. Their attention is not fluid.

This is similar to what happens when you try to roll a drop of water down a dry piece of wood. It has a lot of resistance to rolling. But if you dip your finger into water and create a trail of moisture on the wood—a curvy trail if your wish—and you connect that to the drop, the drop will follow the trail.

In T'ai-chi-Ch'uan, we try to moisten trails within our bodies, trails which naturally exist but may have dried out. These trails are called meridians and serve as natural pathways for attention. (Remember, attention brings nutrients from other levels of body-mind, just as blood brings nutrients from "outside" the body.)

The "boundary" of "your" body-mind, where the other creature takes your pulse of attention and carries it to far realms, where nutrients flow back down the trail to your tan-tien, is not a boundary located in, or defining, physical space. It is a boundary of awareness and varies in its "size" from person to person.

Describing the Dynamics of Attention

The creature that carries your pulse of attention is referred to as the "eagle" in American Indian culture, and the pulse of attention as a "prayer." They say that the eagle carries your prayer to the Great Spirit who then answers your prayer. This is a poetic way of putting it.

My way may sometimes be considered poetic but it is really a mechanical explanation. It is a direct description of the experience. When I first introduce students to the dynamics of attention, they usually tell me they have already experienced this and then proceed, by merely describing their experiences, to tell me what I was going to tell them. Not poetry—direct description of experience. Perhaps you, too, have experienced these things and find that these pages serve to put into words what you already know experientially. Perhaps you just didn't have a language by which to describe these feelings.

That is one reason I use the Gnostic text, *The Gospel of Truth*, to show that almost all cultures (except, perhaps, our own) have a language to describe these experiences. Once you have an experience, you can recognize any description of it. Some historians and anthropologists have written about these ancient texts and actually called these civilizations "primitive"! Fortunately there are also many enlightened anthropologists who open themselves up to the wisdom found in ancient cultures.

Recognizing a Teacher

I have had the good fortune to study with wonderful teachers, people from several cultures who trained me in their ways. Many people have asked me how to find or recognize such a teacher and I believe there is a way. When your attention flows freely through the spiral staircase, the eyes become yin, in the sense that they are open to all they see. They allow whatever they see to flow freely into them, like a pool of water allows a waterfall to flow into it.

Fulfilling Emptiness

Yet the eyes are yang in the sense that there is an evaporation coming from them. You may call it a warmth but it is more like a smell that evaporates from its source; you can sense it, but there is no emotion or meaning in it. In a similar way, evaporation from the eyes allows energy to flow out, just as such a person allows energy to flow in. There is an unimpeding, non-interference quality related to the eyes. This person may seem sad because they refrain from getting caught up in the entanglements of energy of most people. Yet they more appropriately would be called "empty." Emptiness is the unimpeded flow of the complex of energy that is called life. It is a fulfilling emptiness. The part of us that fears this emptiness is what keeps our attention trapped in the everyday games, the emotional highs and lows.

Emptiness allows movement. If all space were filled with matter, nothing could move. The kind of emptiness discussed here allows attention to flow. In Push Hands, I teach students to "fill up the spaces." This means not to concentrate on the force and physical presence of the partner but to concentrate on the empty spaces between the partners. Leave the areas in which the partner is concentrating his force and place your arms and body in the empty spaces which are devoid of his attention. Then you can come in and push. In the spaces that are empty of his attention, you can hide. Then, all of a sudden, you "appear" and push his body.

A type of space can also be filled up with all the assumptions you have made in your life. If you go back and remember how your structure of understanding (of what is going on in this world) was built, and how those assumptions have affected your life, you see that a different set of assumptions would have led to a very different life. The ability to understand that you can change your life by changing your assumptions is a kind of "movement." Allowing for the possibility that alternate assumptions may also be useful is a way of moving through the spaces.

So the issue of emptiness does not imply that a person feels dead or unhappy. This kind of emptiness allows for personal growth. Those who are empty long for others who are empty, not to share sadness but to share unimpeded joy, called "life."

Internal Effects of the Quality of Attention

This joy that one person has for another is the same that one cell in the body has for another. It is the same that one planet has for another. When two such people share their joy, when their attention evaporates from their boundaries to be absorbed by the other, each cell within their bodies duplicates that process. And this process, this union or interpenetration of the attention of two people, reverberates throughout the spiral staircase, both to the higher and the lower floors, as a sound might reverberate throughout a staircase.

Each act of attention is thus a pulse of attention that ripples out in all directions. The dynamics of attention is a serious training with important consequences. It is the essence of T'ai-chi-Ch'uan.

On the negative side, certain patterns of attention, resonating in the cells, can cause serious health problems. The principles of T'ai-chi-Ch'uan describe the most healthful qualities of attention.

For example, the thinking-mind should be yin and body-mind yang. While the body-mind maintains the natural flow of attention, the thinking-mind re-channels this natural flow. Each alteration by the mind produces consequences. This is why the thinking-mind must be yin, so that it doesn't just bludgeon its way through your life. Each alteration must be considered carefully.

Cultural Patterns of Attention

Each culture has its own pattern of attention which gives its citizens certain strengths and weaknesses. When you travel, you see that, while people are basically alike everywhere, there are many behavioral differences among cultures.

At times, the history of how this alteration was developed is lost. In that case the culture no longer understands the origins of its problems or how to avoid problems with a periodic rebalancing of the attention pattern. Yet there is a subconscious awareness on the part of many of its people that such a rebalancing is needed, and so social movements and upheavals are the result.

As an example, years ago we would never have seen a soap commercial in which someone taking a shower would actually touch themselves to wash. They always used a washcloth. There was a tacit understanding that touching your body was against our culture, and seeing it would make people uncomfortable. Soon after the cultural revolution of the '60s began, we saw people in the soap commercials actually touching their bodies. This may not seem like a great innovative change, but it is a deep change, indeed, in our culture. We can learn a lot about cultural change by watching advertisements.

It is not uncommon for a culture to consciously destroy the knowledge of its origin, so the powers that became entrenched after a rebalancing can retain their newfound power.

Our attention pattern, then, is "captured" by the entrenched power. This means that, rather than allowing our attention to flow into other people, into our own bodies, into the natural environment, it is trapped by a pattern of explanations as to what is going on around us. This pattern is the thinking-mind. It occupies the attention, performing tricks and keeping us entertained. No longer can the attention serve to connect the individual with the environment because its flow is stopped.

Death and Re-birth

It doesn't really matter what explanation traps the attention. It could be anything. But the point is that people forget that attention is not the same as thinking. Attention is the lifeblood of the universe, the flowing force that connects everything together, that serves as the medium of communication.

Thinking is a particular skill, one of many. Yet it has become so powerful that some people can't stop thinking. They fear the evaporation of attention as a death. Yet it is a death that leads to re-birth. Once attention is allowed to evaporate, you realize that more comes your way. Attention flows through you and is in unending supply. The fulfillment that comes from reconnecting the channels of attention overpowers the addiction to the mind, as a flood breaks a dam.

Communication Is a Healing Energy

In *The Emerald Forest* the principle of communication (in the form of croaking frogs) helps to flood a river, which breaks a dam. This dam threatens to destroy the forest. (As I remember, it was an eagle that sent the message to all the frogs, to help cause the flood. Consider the meaning of that!)

The dam within you threatens to destroy the forest of life within you. Don't you want someone you can communicate with, just as one cell needs to communicate with the next? What would it be like to share these attention experiences with another person?

When a good teacher looks at other people he wonders, "Is this person a pattern of attention trapped in some side-pool, swirling around forever, or is this person a channel of attention so that the flow of our attentions can merge?" This merging is a physical sensation, like the flowing of momentum in Push Hands or the attention one orchestra player has for the other instruments in the orchestra (to coordinate his instrument with theirs).

When two such people meet, you may imagine they would discuss the subject of attention within some conceptual framework. But instead, their attentions meet and interact, in a Push-Hands kind of way, and they discuss the most mundane things. The words play within their own world while the free flow of attention plays beyond that, and the words become a reflection of the play of attention. This means that ordinary interaction reflects the pattern of attention just as the cellular interactions also reflect these patterns. The pattern of attention, then, is the central issue, and our social behavior, verbal interactions and even the health of the body result from how we channel attention. The mind becomes yin (reflecting the flow of attention through the spiral staircase of body-mind). The mind no longer remains separate from body-mind nor imposes its rigid patterns on body-mind.

Trusting Your Direct Experience

Thinking no longer becomes a search for truth through logic but a reflection of truth, by being a reflection of direct experience. This is like the difference between an armchair philosopher who thinks great thoughts about what is going on in nature and an actual researcher who goes into the field and studies nature firsthand, or performs experiments and studies the results. The researcher's paper in a scientific journal is a reflection of his actual field observations and not just random thoughts that came into his mind one day.

My students ask me, "How will I know that I have experienced such and such?" Others say, "Oh, I know what you're talking about." You can bet that the former are trapped in their minds. They want their minds to validate their experiences. This is an odd thing. How can a reflection of direct experience validate or invalidate the experience itself? If I say that the sun is a bright object in the sky which comes out only during the day and is so bright you can hardly look at it, you would have no trouble knowing what I mean.

Yet it is as if some people ask, "How will I know if I have seen the sun?" In the movie *Dersu Usala*, some surveyors ask a backwoods mountain man in Siberia, "Do you know what the sun is?" He replied, "Yes."

"What do you think it is?" they asked him. He went outside the hut and pointed to it. "That's what it is," he replied.

The Journey of the Eagle

Most of us know about intellectual and geographical journeys. Another kind of journeying is the journey of the eagle. It is as real and significant as the other two. It deals with our health and happiness and our freedom.

Perhaps this may seem like nonsense but most likely, there is something about it that sounds familiar, that seems like it may mean something.

You may experience these very things but if you have not been taught a language to describe it, it is unknown to you. You could deny the experience because it cannot be brought to the mental level. Don't let that cause a problem. Here in this book is a language to use. Search within yourself for experiences that these words seem to describe.

Then we will be able to talk to each other. That tower of Babel—the programmed mind searching for truth through the heights of logic—finally cracks and people believe that they no longer can communicate because they speak different languages. But we can recognize what each other is saying if we don't insist on using the same words. Similarly, I use my own words to convey my experience to you and if you have seen what I have seen, you will know what I'm talking about.

The Power and Importance of the Patterns of Attention

But of what practical use is the dynamic of attention?

Do you know that children would rather provoke their parents to anger against them rather than be ignored? Did you know that a wild animal of a species not prone to socializing will become very social with humans if enough attention is paid to it? Cats are not normally gregarious animals, at least not the type of cat that gave rise to our domestic cats.

What do you think the halo on a picture of a highly considered person actually means? While you look at his face your attention expands to notice the halo. This suggests an expansion of attention, resulting in a peaceful state. We see a pair of eyes that seem to be somewhere else. The attention is yin, which we interpret as a sign of kindness. When the eyes are narrowed and the attention more directed, we get a different feeling.

The religious allegories, such as drawings of spiritual people, really are describing the dynamics of attention.

The Need for Validation of Your Experience

When we dream, our attention expands and pulses move out into other "areas" besides those we have been trained to perceive. Yet we can only comprehend what we have been trained to perceive. The result is that we translate what our little space probe of attention radios back to us as dragons chasing us, interactions with people and the other usual subjects of dreams.

We feel uncomfortable accepting any perception that cannot be explained in words. That is why this book can be used as a vehicle for perception. It provides an intellectual, verbal framework by which to explain perceptions that don't usually have a place in our society. This makes it "safer" to accept what you are already perceiving because it can be talked about.

We are used to having the thinking-mind validate our experiences. But as children, it was our *feelings* that validated our experiences. It was the relationship of an experience to our biological being that determined its "validity." It is the relationship of our biological being to the ecological balance around us that determines the validity of culture in non-technological societies. The optimizing of these relationships leads to health and inner peace for the individual and the society.

So when a person living in an ecologically-oriented culture dreams, the dreaming is as valid as waking. That is, dreaming becomes a way of "sending" ones's attention into biological realms (the workings of the cells in the body, the interactions of the attentions of all manners of living creatures and the interactions of other natural forces).

Counterbalanced Attention

Attention is "bi-planar." It has two aspects. One aspect serves to keep the individual working in harmony with the environment. The other serves to separate the individual from the environment. The separating attention is like centrifugal force in planetary systems. The moon, for example, tends to fly away from the earth. This is equivalent to the thinking-mind. The force of gravity tends to pull the moon toward the earth. This is equivalent to body-mind. The result, as we know, is that the moon orbits the earth.

In our own lives, when our attention is equally spread throughout our biological being and our societal considerations, we have the most balanced lives.

The attention of most people has been so withdrawn from the body and the ecological environment that they are in tremendous imbalance. Perhaps they seek that balance in gaining enlightenment or therapy or dream analysis. They interpret their dreams to mean this or that about themselves.

Other people consider dreams simply nonsensical sequences that happen during sleep. Yet the state of attention when you are dreaming is a vital dynamic of attention. It is the expansive phase, or cycle, of attention, when the energy of attention flows through us most easily. It is when the eagle may most readily carry our pulses of attention off to the fields of nourishment, to browse.

Once we realize this, we become curious as to what these fields of nourishment are like. At this time, the student must develop his repertoire of feelings, which are the experiences of life as seen through the eyes of body-mind.

Expanding Attention

The student must begin to expand his attention. While practicing the Form, he practices beginning the next movement just before the hands float into the proper position for the end of the previous movement. For example, as his arms float to the right in the first turn of "ward off left" (and his weight is on the left leg), he will begin shifting his weight to the right leg *before* his hands are completely in place. In this way, the attention begins to separate and expand. One part of the attention must be on the hands completing their movement, while another part of the attention must be on the weight already shifting to the next movement. Care must be taken for these two parts of the attention to remain connected to each other, so the Form doesn't become disjointed. The result of practicing the Form in this way will be a flowing, elastic appearance.

In dreamwork, the student first splits his attention between the dream and the experience of his body lying in the bed. This allows him to then divide his attention between the dream images and the feeling associated with each image. In this way his attention can expand, to be aware of two types of things at the same time.

Then he drops the images of dragons, etc., and substitutes images of artistic patterns (with no meaning to those patterns) to represent the feelings. This is done after the student is quite familiar with freestyle Push Hands. He uses his experience with Push Hands in the following way:

1. He can notice in the patterns or in the feelings themselves (arising out of dreamwork) various interactions taking place.
2. From Push-Hands experience, he knows that such swirls, eddies and

currents of feeling must be produced by the interaction of individual but connecting wills (as in the wills of the Push Hands partners).

3. The artistic patterns (which are visual translations of his feelings) help him discern the "feeling location" of each such will. That is, he infers from the resulting patterns which parts of his feelings represent the origins of the interactions.

Imagine two pebbles dropped into a still pond. They create a circular series of ripples, which interact. By seeing this complex pattern, you can infer where each of the two pebbles were dropped.

Increasing the Resolution of Attention

In the body, there are not just two pebbles, but an enormous number of organs, cells, molecules and atoms, each very active.

So usually we only get a general sense of their workings. It is as if we listened to an orchestra. At first we only hear one general sound. Then we begin to pick out individual instruments. Then we notice how these instruments interact with each other.

This is similar to the process of discerning the patterns of feeling within the body. The interactions of the patterns become a hologram, encoding much information about the structure and functioning of the individual wills that gave rise to the hologram.

Each cell, each molecule has its own will, its own nature, its own way of reacting, its own Tao. The activity of each will creates the eddies and currents in the field of attention.

By pulsing spherical waves of attention outward from the tan-tien (the balancing center of body-mind and the central focus of attention), you are illuminating the eddies and currents of the hologram (as long as the pulses are not lumpy).

The Cycles of Cellular Wills

But this pulsing also does something far more important. On each in-breath (each pulse outward), the body-mind—the communication system among all the cells—is pulled taut, in a sense so that the functioning of each cell and molecule is made to "line up" more in harmony with the others. On each out-breath, the individual wills of the cells are allowed their individuality, their freedom.

Now at this point, consider this last idea. Do some breathing and notice whether this seems true according to your feelings. Do your guts say, "He's right!," or not? You can sense, for example, that there is more to the act of yawning than bringing air into the lungs. You can *feel* there's more to it.

When you pulse a spherical wave of attention out on the in-breath, the eagle carries it beyond your boundary to the next level of body-mind. There it connects to that level so that all the individual cells of the body line up in their functioning, not only to the rest of the body, but to the ecological environment. Stand in a beautiful natural area and notice how you feel while breathing in, as compared to breathing out.

Breath is, in a manner of speaking, like a pump of attention, pulsating down to the most minute levels on the out-breath and up to the grandest levels on the in-breath.

There are slower cycles as well. In the dreaming state, as with an in-breath, the attention expands beyond the boundaries. The waking state is characterized by a focusing of attention. This slower cycle is superimposed over the faster breathing cycle.

Then there is an even slower cycle of what we know as life—a focusing, and death—a diffusion of attention.

Attention is the very spirit of life. Its dynamics determine the quality of our lives. Since attention is so intimately connected to breath, the practice of gaining the skill of the dynamics of attention is sometimes referred to as "spirit breathing" and this is the term I use in my teachings.

I have often felt that if all I do in my life is keep the teaching of spirit breathing alive, then my life will serve an important purpose.

Shallow breathers go neither out, to align the individual wills of body-mind, nor in, to free up those wills. Thus this natural cycle, designed to keep us healthy and at peace, is very weak.

Notice when you just wake up but are still in that twilight world, how the breath is deep and slow and how the dream images move in pace with the breath.

Uniting the Dreaming and Waking States

During sleep, we make up for shallow breathing and reconnect to the cycle of attention. The T'ai-chi Form gives us the same benefit. All our movements in the Form are coordinated with slow, deep breathing. All movement of the body is at an even pace and the attention flows smoothly.

During the Form, when we breathe in, momentum emanates out of the body (usually out the palms, but in a general sense, spherically out of the entire body). Our attention, sitting at the crest of the wave of momentum, flows out with it. This teaches us to allow our attention out of the body.

We go a step further now and learn to practice the Form in our dreams. Likewise, when awake and physically practicing the Form, we allow dream images to come up so that part of us is "dreaming."

Thus we are uniting the dreaming state and waking state, or rather, we are bringing together two practices (dreaming and the Form) which emphasize the flow of attention through the spiral staircase. This is how teachers try to push the students into that flow.

In some cultures you are taught to imagine a point on the ground. Breathing in is like a cone extending from that point upward to greater levels of body-mind. Breathing out is a cone extending from the spot downward to finer and finer levels of body-mind. The plane of the ground itself is our everyday practical lives, the stage upon which our lives are played. The breath flows past this point like sand in an hourglass.

This central "point" is not something located in three-dimensional space as if one could search for it. It is a point one can "find" with the flow of attention. It is a "place" the attention can go or rather, qualities the attention can attain. It is called "the gate."

With the dreaming and waking states united, the discernment of "real" or "unreal" is no longer related to waking or dreaming ("reality" or "illusion"). It is related to the activities and interactions that take place on and among the various levels of body-mind. A perception is useful if it gives you information about those interactions.

This is not what one would call "getting too immersed in yourself." A person's connection to all other things, including the earth, is a central issue. The one thing it does seem to do is make it difficult to engage in "small talk." Such banter becomes uninteresting and even difficult to understand. Usual human interactions, centered around issues of self-worth, control and power in a social sense, become bewildering to a person involved in spirit breathing. The purpose and benefit of such interaction becomes unclear when viewed from the perspective of body-mind.

This perspective does not include the idea "I am better than you because. . . ." It is a perspective of connecting and unifying rather than overpowering.

Health Effects of the Cycles of Cellular Will

Remember that the attention dynamics on the individual level reflect and affect dynamics on a cellular level. When we breathe out, the attention goes to "the center." Yet this center does not just mean the tan-tien. It means that the attention can move to the centers of each and every cell of the body. In this way, the attention is decentralized into the constituent wills of the body.

If an individual is pathologically independent (to the point where his need for independence hurts him) this may be reflected in his breathing. He may feel much more confident breathing out and keeping his breath low and shallow. Someone who is pathologically dependent and is afraid to exert his own will may feel more confident breathing in and may keep the breath more high up in the chest, also in a shallow way. Thus you may find people with puffed-out chests more comfortable being part of a military-type organization, where they can feel like cogs in a wheel. This may be the opposite of what you would expect. Somehow we think of people with puffed-out chests as independent.

The yin and yang aspects of any interaction are inseparable. Each can only exist as a reflection of the other. When the attention of each cell expands, as it exerts its will, it meets with the will of the cells around it and is thus restricted in its independence. As its energy drops back into its center, as its will is let go, it can then actually function more independently because its will no longer meets with the resistance of the other cells.

This is reflected on an individual level as well. In T'ai-chi we learn that in order to be effective in Push Hands or fighting, we must not interfere with the other person's will. Let them punch at the location occupied by your face, but remove your face from that location before the fist lands in that spot. Giving up the desire to control the movements of the other person allows you to be more effective and actually to be in control of the interaction.

When we breathe fully in and out, we are balancing the exertion of will and the connectedness with other beings.

In the above fighting situation, we do not merely duck the punch but we return the strike as we duck. In this way we also balance our exertion of will with our connectedness (flowing out of his way).

A specialist in Chinese medicine can tell a lot about a person by the way he breathes. Each variation of breathing reflects a susceptibility of the body to certain kinds of diseases.

Effect of the Cycles of Cellular Will on Relationships

Similarly, one's method of interacting with others reflects one's inner condition. Conversation can be an exchange of information or an attempt to control the behavior and opinions of others. The balance of these two ways of interacting reflects a like condition in the cells and the balance of power of mind and body-mind.

Mind is really the perspective of the single individual while body-mind is the perspective of the community of beings making up that individual.

A person who stays at a central level of breath (not very far down or up) but breathes shallowly is not healthy. He never allows the cells to fully deal with their particular independent situation nor does he allow the cells to fully line up with the other cells and harmonize their activities.

Imagine a relationship of two people in which the attention of one reaches down into the very cells of the other, into their centers. On the reverse cycle of breathing, the other person's attention reaches fully down into the cells of the first. Thus the two are truly united on a body-mind level and their love is organic.

The problem with attaining this ideal relationship is that too often, the internal condition of one person is not in harmony. One person might subconsciously want to unite with the other so they unite on a body-mind level. In this case, the healthier of the two will have a healing effect on the unhealthy one, often losing some of his own well-being in the process.

This results in a feeling of being drained by the other person. Yet when the less healthy person is healed, he or she will no longer have a use for the healthier one and will want to break off the relationship. This is parasitism and most of us have experienced it either as parasite or victim. Then, as a victim, we wonder what we did wrong to cause the other to close up against us? When a leech gets its belly full of blood, it no longer needs its victim until its next meal. (It is no wonder we become anemic.)

Interference with the Cycle of Cellular Will

There are other forces that interfere with the connectedness/independence cycle of the cells. Whatever grabs our attention and manipulates it affects the cells. It may be another person, television, our work, or even habits within us such as patterns of thinking. We may not be able to extricate ourselves from some of these influences (such as a job) and that is why T'ai-chi comes in handy. The daily Form gives us at least twenty minutes or so during which our cells can go through their natural attention cycles.

To avoid getting caught up in influences that disrupt this cycle severely, we practice another attention dynamic. When switching from one point of concentration to another, we first return the focus of our attention to the center (to the tan-tien and from there to the centers of the cells). In this way, even though this focus may remain out during several in- and out-breaths in order to pay attention, we do not go for long without going through at least one cycle.

When breathing out, the independent cells are, in a sense, demanding that the environment conform to their needs. They draw the "attention" of the environment into themselves.

Thus when someone remains near the bottom (out-breath) of the breathing cycle with the associated relaxation, the attention of others is drawn to that person. But should the same person remain near the top (in-breath) of the cycle, with the associated puffed-out chest and rising shoulders, this may be perceived as a threat and the attention of the other people will "tense up" into a resistance. They will feel competitive.

In this way, people are acting like cells.

Spotlighting the Cells

The next attention dynamic deals with becoming aware of the cellular activities. We already read that pulsing an even, smooth pulse of attention outward can act like a spotlight, making the activity patterns of the cells more visible. This is because the activities of the cells (and organs and molecules) create eddies and currents in the field of attention.

On the out-breath, we then send the attention to the centers of each cell. This is something that happens naturally. If we can follow our attention all the way down to this level, we can notice that the cells "grab" and use the attention energy. They are like baby birds being fed by the mother. The way in which they grab at and use the attention reveals their nature. This is something that can be felt, in the same way a sudden sound tugs at your attention.

(Notice the image of the cells as baby birds grabbing for attention, and compare that to "the eagle" (adult eagle) carrying your attention to the "Great Spirit" among American Indians. Can you use these two poetic descriptions to guide you to be aware of these experiences within yourself?)

I find that I have to remain in the out-breath for at least fifteen to thirty seconds to have enough time to be aware of this interaction (of the cells and the attention).

The next step is to keep your attention down at the cellular level on both the in-breath and out-breath. You will still be sending pulses outward but the attention, previously centered in the tan-tien, will now be centered at a lower level of body-mind. In a sense, you will be sending your periscope down to the cellular level.

Learning the Cellular Culture

This will have a profound effect on your personality (as will centering the attention on an ecological level). This is so because you will be aware of how each interaction in your life affects the cells.

It is as if someone knew little about a group of people and then lived with them awhile. He would then have an appreciation for how these people think and perceive the world around them. The people, in this case, are the cells.

After practicing this style of spirit breathing, your interactions with other people will be operating from a deeper level.

On the other hand, with the periscope on the next higher level, you will be aware of yourself as a cell of the earth. Your social interactions will be coming from a deeper level in that sense, too.

Becoming Truly Whole

Eventually "your" attention can fill up the entire spiral staircase while being aware of all the individual interactions at each floor. Then again, "you" may zero in on a specific level and a specific will to play out a specific life. At this point, of course, there is really no individuality of attention. We should rather speak of the attention of the earth going into individuals and individualizing.

As a single human we can thus get a taste of our connection to the whole of life and how we can participate in that whole.

These experiences are not superhuman, or only meant for a few great masters. Rather, they are the ordinary experiences of life, felt by every living organism. But we humans, not having the words for these experiences, behave as if we don't have them. We don't have our thinking-mind's permission to experience what is right in front of us.

CHAPTER 12
NATURE AND THE POWER OF ATTENTION

Having worked with animals all my life, I have come to know a variety of consciousnesses. You have to know the consciousness of an animal in order to deal with it. This has led me to appreciate the "continuum of consciousnesses," that is, the whole range of consciousnesses possible, each just slightly different from the next.

Understanding the nature of the differences and variations of the qualities of the consciousnesses also helps you to understand their underlying commonality, a commonality shared by me and you. This has given me a hint as to the nature of the consciousness of the whole earth, of all of life.

With any vertebrate creature, certainly those closest to us, there is a recognition of other forms of vertebrate life as aware beings. When I see another animal and we look at each other, there is a recognition and then a wondering of intention, a sizing up of power. That sizing up is based on certain criteria. Can he overpower me and eat me? Does he want to? Can I eat him? Is he benign?

These can be described as common characteristics of consciousness. Our subsequent behavior toward each other emanates from this initial sizing up.

A similar process happens when an organism encounters its environment. The sizing-up process and subsequent behavior determines to a large extent the fulfillment of the potential of the organism. Isn't it the fulfillment of our potential, in all areas of our life, that brings us joy? T'ai-chi-Ch'uan is a discipline that can lead us to such joy by explaining our own lives in terms of nature.

Joy—Nature at Work

Within a fertilized cell or the seed of a plant lies a pattern for the fully mature organism. Given time and proper environmental conditions, a person, tree or zebra is formed. The growth of that organism as the unraveling of its inner patterns is what I mean by the term "joy."

"Joy" in this sense implies nature proceeding along its natural cycles, for the seed is but one part of an endless series of cycles—tree, seed, sprout, tree, seed, etc.

There are many levels of such patterns and their cyclic growth. A tree is one. But the forest itself may have a natural succession, a natural growth of its own. First, lichens begin to transform rocks to soil. Then small plants may grow, then bushes, low trees and finally, tall trees. The nature of the forest's plant and animal population changes as the forest grows. Then the earth itself may go through changes, such as climatic changes.

The sciences of biology and ecology impress on us that all these cycles and patterns are interrelated. They are geared to each other. Even the atmosphere and resultant weather are felt to be largely influenced by biological activity and the production of gases by organic life.

Within our bodies, each organ, each meal we eat and each movie we watch has an effect on the overall well-being of the body. Our mental attitudes, tension, relaxation, anger, have physical effects on the body.

Our living planet, of which we are part, is a whole integrated system in which the smallest pattern or cycle is connected to the largest.

In this way, any healing directed to even one small part of the planet, such as an attitude within your own mind, causes some degree of healing to the entire planet. Healing yourself is effective in healing the planet, as is working to preserve a forest. Working to preserve a forest can be as healing to you as directly healing yourself.

The T'ai-chi practice of Chi-gung is largely concerned with healing. One of the main concerns of this practice is to strengthen the connections among the various levels of organic life both within yourself, and between you as an individual and the living planet around you. This, in itself, is a healing process.

Attention and Survival

As we evolved into multicellular organisms, attention was decentralized in one respect. Each cell and each group of cells had to have a fair share of the energy of the entire organism to function. It had to have fair access to the resources of communication in order to coordinate its functions with those of the other cells.

Should any type of cell or any area of the multicellular organism be deprived of such access, its activities would fall out of harmony with the rest of the organism.

For example, those sense organs receiving information from the "outside environment" are as important as those receiving information about the organism's internal state. In this way, the internal state can alter and adjust to the external environment. The internal state can be adjusted well in advance of when factors outside would actually affect the organism.

For example, a prey species can run away from a predator as soon as the predator is sighted, rather than waiting for the first bite. Birds can migrate long before the cold weather sets in.

There are cues in the external environment that warn an organism to alter its behavior physically and chemically. So the organism must have at least two major centers of awareness, or two internal controlling factors of its behavior. One recognizes a proper state (proper chemical composition of blood, internal temperature, etc.) and the other recognizes cues which may eventually challenge that state. Perhaps a third part knows what to do to avoid interference with the proper state of being.

The speed of internal communication determines the organism's efficiency and survival. This lesson is made clear to us in T'ai-chi kickboxing. Very often, when we are tired, we will see that punch coming into our face but we have only an eighth of a second or so to react. Our tiredness interferes with the internal communications and responses. We can almost hear our bodies saying, "Yes, I know it's coming, but I'm too tired to do anything about it." The fighting vivifies the network of internal communications, resulting in greater overall health.

The internal communication network is attention. Attention is what connects one thing to another. It draws things to itself. When you love someone, you pay attention to that person. When you hear a loud sound and turn toward it quickly, you search for its source and try to connect with it, to know what it is.

Gravity is the earth's attention because it holds us to her. She draws us to her center with the force of gravity. The cells are connected to each other through attention. Conscious organisms are connected to each other through attention.

When a cell no longer functions in accordance with the rest of the body and no longer functions to enhance the well-being of the body, we say that it is parasitic, acting only on its own behalf. We say it is cancerous. It is no longer connected to the other cells through the force of attention. Thus, attention is an important issue.

The Quality of Attention

Since attention permeates all levels of our being, the pattern or quality of attention is very important. If, on the level of an individual organism, we are disconnected and act in a way to emphasize our separation from others (ego), then this quality will echo throughout the cellular level as well, creating health problems.

If, on the other hand, we keep in mind the dynamics of attention required to maintain the body's health and try to translate that into our everyday interactions, we can maximize our health.

Notice through the day what you pay attention to. How much attention is on the internal body activity, as compared with the senses, as compared with thoughts, as compared with physical sensations? Is your attention mainly concentrated in one part of the body—the head, the stomach, the feet—where?

When you are startled or when your attention is distracted, does all or most of your attention go to the distraction or only a portion of the attention? What kinds of things draw your attention most readily?

How do cues in the external environment affect your behavior, your mood?

We multicellular organisms are, in turn, cells of a larger organism, the earth. We communicate within our own species, using language, body language, books, electronic media, et al. There is also communication between species. The deer knows if the predator is hunting it or just passing by, by subtle behavior on the part of the predator.

Systems of attention exist among all the cells of the earth. Energies of many forms flow in endless cycles. Cues in the environment tell us the state of the entire earth organism and what we must do to function for its benefit. Were we to neglect these cues and our responsibilities, we would be a cancer of the earth. Anything which robs humans of attention or distracts us from paying attention to the proper state of the earth organism will result in the illness of the earth.

Teaching the Dynamics of Attention

Unfortunately, such cues do not fall within the realm of words. They are directly experienced by each individual. Words can only describe exercises which lead you to the experiences. They can point to building blocks of your life you never noticed were there. They can suggest other arrangements of those blocks that will finally give you the power to make changes in your life you may have assumed were impossible to achieve.

CHAPTER 13
ATTENTION EXERCISES

Are intelligence and creativity part of ourselves or are they energies of the earth that flow through us?

Are all the thoughts we think part of ourselves or are they a form of "thought scenery" that we pay attention to? Are they a distraction or do we generate them? Are thoughts confined to the three-dimensional space of our bodies or are they free to move out of ourselves to be received by other people?

The implications of such questions are enormous. But the result of understanding gained by exploring them is a clarity, a freedom, a sense of belonging and a union with life.

EXERCISE 1—THE JOLT OF THOUGHT

Whenever you think a thought in your mind, try not to translate it into words. When a spark or jolt of thought hits you—a feeling that you are about to think something, concentrate on that feeling. Let go of the need to translate it into words. Stay with the initial jolt rather than with the words.

You will find that the entire idea is contained within that initial jolt. The words are a slow, cumbersome translation for the benefit of the thinking-mind.

If you learn to "think" with the jolts rather than needing to translate into words, your mind will be freed of clutter without disregarding anything of value.

This jolt is like a seed. It contains within itself the entirety of the message. Any translation is a simplification of the original seed. This means that words can only vaguely approximate some of the meaning of the original seed or jolt.

If you pay attention to the words and not to the seed, you will lose most of the message. When you give up the words, you gain the ability to perceive more information from the seed. This seed contains many implications, many possible unfoldments, just as a child may have many possible futures depending on opportunities. The word *translation* is but one interpretation of the seed. It thus blocks out all but one implication, blinding us to the others.

In many ways, we pay attention to the translation of potent messages and potent communications, rather than to the seeds, and lose vitality and vigor, mentally and physically.

T'ai-chi teaches us many ways to discover the power inherent in our internal communications and how to become aware of them. The Form itself is a seed. It contains within itself a lifetime of lessons. Yet it is only a fifteen- or twenty-minute series of movements.

Many cultures have created such seeds, such potent patterns of communication. These seeds are really a representation of the patterns of communication within us, and between us as individuals and the rest of nature. They are instructions as to how to align oneself in harmony with this immense pattern of communication.

Anyone who has been trained even a little in such a system can't help but be awed by the insight of innumerable teachers throughout the centuries whose goal was to bring "joy" to their students and to the earth.

Becoming Attuned to Your Seeds

Yet the real teaching begins when one listens to that communication. The body, the earth, a tree, will reveal to you valuable information. Human teachings can only show you how to listen: What you will hear when you listen is personal to yourself, privileged information meant for your own ears.

When you are able to tune in to the jolt, notice how different jolts or information seeds feel. Their differences of feeling are a way for you to know them and read them. Read with your feelings rather than with your logic. You will discover that each seed-feeling is complex and contains much information. You must learn to develop a high resolution of feeling—the ability to detect the slightest differences in feeling. The finer your ability the more information you will gain.

You also need to narrow your time experience, as in fighting, to increase resolution. The more changes you can detect per second as your partner shifts from one position to the next, the more appropriately you will be able to respond. This is the same as in digital audio recording. If you can record the pitch and volume only 1,000 times per second, the result will be poor. But if you can record this information 1,000,000 times per second or more, the results will be very listenable.

I used to breed mice to sell to pet shops. In one cage, there were twenty-five to thirty babies and I had to grab each one by the tail and place it in a shipping container. When the customer orders five hundred mice, you try to grab as quickly as possible or it could take all day. Imagine thirty mice all running around quickly as mice do and you have to reach in and grab the tiny tail. You must be skilled enough to use only one grab to catch a mouse. This was excellent training for increasing the resolution of concentration.

The old video games of shooting down enemy space creatures also developed this resolution. Catching fish with bare hands was an old training method in Chinese kung-fu schools. You can think of other such exercises. Then use that ability on a feeling level with the jolt of thought.

You must analyze or "see" these seed-feelings quickly because they last only a moment. These jolts are part of the interaction between the perception of the organism (person) and the resultant reaction of the cells of the body. It is part of the process of communication and it takes place on a much faster time scale than we are used to.

If we could tune in to that process, we would see the process of our own growth in relation to the growth of the earth. We would be tuning in to joy.

Animal Joy

Have you ever wondered what fun animals get out of life? Most of them just eat, mate, sleep, etc., and except perhaps for a few, like otters, don't seem to take time out to have fun.

An answer to this question came to me one day when I brought my canoe under a tree overhanging a jungle river in Panama. I love to travel alone in the jungle and I was on a research/camping trip. It had begun to rain and the tree provided some protection. As I sat in the canoe with a plastic sheet over my head, I watched the monkeys, birds and reptiles. They sat, staring across the river as if in meditation or prayer. I looked across the river, trying to feel what they were getting out of this experience.

The river, Rio Chepo, was about one hundred feet wide and thickly lined with jungle trees. Large raindrops poured down onto the muddy water. The resultant sound created a feeling of expectation, as if the rain were an orchestra tuning up for a symphony.

I sat for perhaps two hours until I realized that my normal process of attention had changed. The act of sitting, listening to the rain, staring across the river, was as significant, fulfilling, purposeful as the act of eating or writing, mowing the lawn or paddling a canoe. Yet, logically, I couldn't figure out the purpose. What did it accomplish?

Then I looked at an iguana sitting on a branch above me and to my right. It calmly turned its head toward me so it could see me with its left eye. Then it turned its gaze back to the river, and so did I.

But the experience of that singular look was as revealing as the teachings of any human teacher I have met—more so. (My work with animals since almost my birth has given me innumerable such moments, more than enough reward for my work in the field of environmental conservation.)

Now, I will try to explain the iguana's look and my new understanding resulting from that experience. That look was a seed—a very beautiful, complex seed, though my translation into words cannot do it justice.

Firstly, I felt in no uncertain terms that in the degree of awareness, the iguana was at least my equal. It looked at me with an inner strength and confidence I could only admire. Its look reached through my eyes deep into my body and heart and, to describe it poetically, illuminated something inside me.

It was a level of awareness in which every part of my experience—my body, my senses (external and internal), thoughts, feelings, etc., were equal. They were equal in importance, in their identity to me, in their creatureness. Each experience—iguana, thought, body, rock—was sentient, communicated, felt.

I was being addressed by each of these innumerable things and part of me, a part "I" hardly knew, communicated back. I turned to the iguana again and it turned to me. I could swear that it smiled, though iguanas do not smile. Perhaps I should say that I felt it knew that I knew. At that moment, my mind "saved me" from this sentimentality and suggested that if the iguana was so "equal" to me that I move toward it to see if it were self-confident enough not to run away. (Iguanas run away at the slightest hint of approach.)

I immediately took myself up on my suggestion. Yet I found that the level on which I "connected to" the iguana remained stronger than my logic. As I stood up and began to move toward the iguana, I felt as if I were performing a ritual movement of acknowledgement. That is, I moved toward it but not in a threatening way. We stared at each other for a few moments and then I sat down again. (The iguana was about eight feet from me and they usually run when you get to within twenty-five feet.)

I thought of my logic at that moment as one would think of an obnoxious, ignorant person—one who thought too much of himself.

Seeds—Paths to Joy

I stared out over the river. Its muddy water seemed like a giant blood vessel running through the body of the jungle. The jungle's moisture and warmth joined me to it. The cleverness of my logic did not seem as valuable as it always had.

I longed to see, to feel, to communicate with this warm living ecosystem more than to know facts about it. Up to that point, I had wanted to work in the field of biological research. Now, the seed of another path was beginning to sprout.

Think of the "jolt" of your thought as the look of the iguana. When it first looked at me, I moved my head back a few inches and opened my mouth as if someone had told me something very surprising, something I must take seriously. The seeds you will experience, the jolts, are of this nature. They reveal paths to joy.

And these jolts are right here with us, as if so many iguanas, sitting on branches all around us. If we try to grab these jolts by concentrating on them in an aggressive way, they will surely escape. Notice them with a feeling of respect. Don't try to grab them with your logic but just feel them, see them and learn from them.

They speak in a different language. They communicate with a different part of yourself. Their message is harmony.

EXERCISE 2—EXPAND ATTENTION

Notice the inconsequential. As we experience our world, we often fail to notice most of our experience. We are searching or scanning the world to find a specific item.

The farmer searches the sky to determine tomorrow's weather. Someone at a party will search for a possible mate. A tense person will search for the opportunity for an argument.

For many of us, the world echoes our expectation. The world we notice reflects what we expect to find. Yet, of course, the world is so much more. The pattern of expectation we carry with us creates a vision of the world that is an outward representation of our inner behavior, attitudes and thoughts, thus the notion "echo of expectation."

As long as we search the world for what we expect to find, we will not truly see the world. Then, factors that escape our notice will not be taken care of. These neglected parts of our lives will build up until they interfere with our lives so strongly that we can no longer ignore them. Then we will say, "How did that happen? Just my bad luck."

Many people know they are at high risk for a heart attack. They drink a lot of coffee, smoke a lot of cigarettes and never exercise. They may even feel some of the warning signals. Yet often it takes the heart attack itself to catch their attention. We know intellectually that the earth is being destroyed. Yet as long as our lawns are green we take little action. Paying attention and noticing what is going on around us implies taking responsibility for our lives, for the earth. It implies effort.

Perhaps more importantly, a world consisting only of echoes of our expectation is bland and unfulfilling. If we notice the world around us, our lives will be enriched.

Subjective Longevity

It is said that T'ai-chi increases longevity. This is true not only in the number of years lived, but also in subjective time. If we can only notice something that remains in our field of awareness for several seconds or more, we will miss much. If we only notice things which are very bright, loud or harsh, we will miss even more.

A person who can notice the small, short-lived, soft, empty, will live in a vaster, "longer" world. If he notices something every second, his life will seem twice as long as that of someone who can only notice things every two seconds.

In the kickboxing practice, we have to notice changes in our partner's posture, position, balance, etc., ten times each second. If our partner can only notice changes and react to them five times a second, then we are twice as fast as he and see twice as much.

Then when we go back to our everyday activities, we notice so much more, that we previously neglected. Kickboxing helps to increase our subjective longevity.

Furthermore, it teaches us that we must pay attention to the moment. Our full attention must be on that one-tenth second of time. At the next moment, we must let go of the previous one-tenth second and now concentrate fully on this one.

Eventually we reach a state which some people call the "eternal now," in which your attention is fully on the immediate present at every moment. Your attention flows like water and permeates every part of yourself as water moistens the earth and can even seep into hard rocks.

Each moment is an eternity because your attention is fully in it and seeps into every part of your awareness, whether "significant" or "insignificant." Your attention joins you to the world.

No longer do you spend so much effort trying to escape the moment by living in the past or future. No longer do you try to escape the things of the world by judging what is important enough to be deserving of your attention.

Notice within yourself the activity of disassociating yourself from those inner feelings you judge to be "bad." How does this act of disassociation affect your joy?

When a Zen master was asked, "What is Zen?," he answered, "That dried dung."

Open Your Awareness

This exercise consists of simply noticing the seemingly inconsequential—sights, sounds, feelings, thoughts, etc. Notice and then move on. Don't get caught up in what you notice. A gum wrapper lying in the street, an insect sound, the smell of water, the experience of a thought capturing your attention, the feeling of air against your skin, someone's facial expression and your emotional reaction to that expression.

Along with this exercise is what I call three T'ai-chi principles: See yourself, be yourself and appreciate yourself. See all that you are, without judgement, just with clarity. Then feel free to be that which you see, without the inner coercion that warps you into a predetermined shape. Then appreciate the long path of learning that led you to this point in life. Appreciate the effort you put into surviving and learning.

Of course, there's room for improvement, but appreciation comes first.

Then do the same with the "world." See it, all of it. See it without judgement but with clarity. Then be it. Accept your entire world, all you experience, as a whole system of life of which you are part. Then appreciate it, not only the natural world, but all the effort and creativity we humans have put into developing our culture, technology, minds, art.

Of course, there's room for improvement, but appreciation (letting go of anger and self-righteousness) comes first.

By noticing the inconsequential, you will be noticing all that lies beyond your echo of expectation; you will see the world.

By not judging what you see, not shutting out of your awareness what you judge to be inconsequential, you will cease to separate yourself from the world. After all, consequential really means how important, how related it is, to you. If all your world is equally related to you, it is you.

Once you stop separating yourself from the world, you can appreciate the world and yourself because they are identical. The past, present, future, inside, outside, self, other, mind, body converge. This point, the place of this convergence, is creativity, the ultimate seed.

EXERCISE 3—PASSIVE OBSERVER

Watching without comment. Walking through a carnival, loud with barkers, vying for your business, your attention, you walk by, smiling, observing, inwardly calm.

"I will give you three shots for a dollar," says one of the carnival barkers. Another offers four. Still another, five.

One barker offers a large stuffed animal as a prize for getting three shots out of four. Another offers an even larger prize for only two shots out of four. And so it goes, until you hear an offer you can't refuse.

But then comes an even better offer. "One shot out of four for the biggest prize." It's a great offer but there's a catch. If you lose, you have to give up your health or your freedom or your growth or your dignity or all of the above. If you refuse to play, you must leave the carnival.

There are several things you can do. 1. Leave. 2. Play. 3. Question the rules. 4. Refuse to abide by the rules. 5. Ignore the barker who proposes this arrangement. 6. Bop the barker on the head. 7. Pay attention to the barker but don't respond in any way.

Awareness Without Comment

We will use option 7 for this exercise. The barker is all of the things that capture our attention—sights, sounds, thoughts, feelings, smells, worries, etc. We will notice how our attention jumps from one thing to another but will not get caught up in the game of any of them, no matter how enticing, no matter how great the reward, no matter how great the threat. We will allow our attention to move as quickly and frequently from one thing to another as it so desires, as quickly as the barkers are able to capture it.

Yet there will be a center from which all this observation takes place. Remaining at the center is essential to allow the attention its free movement. This process will strengthen the center and strengthen the freedom of movement of the attention.

Attention will become smooth with nothing for the barker to grab hold of. It will become light, clear, resilient and alive.

And so will the body. The human body forms from the pattern of attention. The body is a form of joy, the unfolding of a natural cycle, and the pattern of attention implanted by creativity regulates that unfolding.

Attention is the communication of how that process of unfolding is doing. (Barkers try to become a substitute pattern and to implant that pattern in your attention.)

Earth's Creativity Flows Through You

This exercise allows the attention to become disentangled from the barkers' snares (by smiling at each and then moving on) and centers the attention into the next level of creativity. The first level is our own personal creativity. The next level is the creativity of the earth. Our own creativity may be thought of as a hole, a tiny emptiness, through which the creativity of the earth pours forth.

In this way, we are a seed of the earth and our own growth, and activity has relevance only in harmony with the natural cycles of the earth. Our lives are an unfolding of a seed of the earth.

The human race has experimented with closing that hole, that emptiness, and so has lost much of its original power, joy and creativity.

We feel we can disregard the dynamics of our connection to the earth and thus we do as we wish. We have searched for another type of seed, another pattern to serve as the basis for our lives, to unfold through our lives.

And this search has led us to various theories, mathematics and religions which now serve as the basis for our behavior. We look to the thinking-mind for the seeds and, rather than creativity empowering (flowing through) the seed, it is individual will that serves this purpose.

This is a change chronicled in many mythologies and most notably in the conflict between the Catholic Christians and the Gnostics.

The Ten Thousand Things

To give a better feeling for this change, let's think of it in a more down-to-earth way. Someone is involved in a relationship and wants to feel in control. They don't want their partner to get the better of them. The dynamics of the relationship are based on getting as much as possible and giving as little as possible. Soon, each act is calculated and not spontaneous. A mental image is created about the intentions, integrity and motivations of the partner. One's own behavior is controlled by this image of the partner.

The relationship is soon taking place between the two images (one in each person concerning the other person) rather than between the two people. Each person has then created two images (one of the other person and one which is the corresponding self-image—the pattern of behavior which stems from the image of the partner). One has created the two and the two (the interactions between these images), the "ten thousand things" (the echoes of expectation which constitute one's personal world).

Life is lived to fulfill these expectations rather than to fulfill the natural original self.

The new seed which unfurls through your life is the thinking-mind—the ten thousand expectations, which form the structure of one's world.

And every cell in your body wonders, "Hey! When did we vote for this change?" Of course, no vote was taken. This was not a conscious, well-thought-out change, but an unconscious attempt to fit into one's culture, to survive as a cultural being.

Reconnecting to the Earth

This exercise is designed to give you a tool that will enable you to see what you've done. You will understand the mechanism that disconnects you from the earth and connects you to a structure of thinking, to the barker's barks. You will learn how each thought affects the body biologically and affects even your perception of the world around you.

You will learn which of the barkers walked over to you, put his arm around your shoulder (as if he were your friend) and led you to his game. You will see the effect that game had on your life and gain the strength to let that game go.

You will learn the difference between being the winner of a game and being aware and alive.

Have we as a society won the game of knowledge only to have poisoned ourselves, threatened ourselves with nuclear annihilation, lost our health and joy? Our particular form of knowledge is a game at a carnival. We hope to win a bigger and bigger stuffed animal but forget to get on with our lives. The game became our lives and we would give up all for it. To win is thus to lose.

In T'ai-chi-Ch'uan we say that to lose is to win and we mean that letting go of the game helps us gain our lives.

Let the Attention Go

So in this exercise we first feel ourselves as a center, a home base for our attention. The attention is like a teacher's pointer, pointing first to this and then to that. But the teacher maintains his hold on the pointer.

Consider all you perceive as scenery. Thoughts are scenery that is already there, just as are sights. Feelings, your body movements, sensations, whatever your attention goes to, are scenery that exists whether or not you pay attention to it. Do not interfere with your attention either by keeping it on anything or taking it away.

Recognize no inner or outer, no self or other. All scenery is equal in importance. (Find a quiet, safe place to do this and a specially set-aside amount of time.) Judge nothing, only passively observe as if nothing had any meaning.

You may find your attention "sticking" to a thought or sight and you must learn how to get your attention so smooth that nothing will stick to it.

The Effects of Freed Attention

A strange peace may seep into your life, the relaxation of turbulence. The world around you may seem fresher, more alive and your senses will be sharper. You will notice much more of the world and simpler things will satisfy you. You may feel as if your nerve system has grown into the world and that you can sense objects around you as if they were part of your own body.

When your attention is no longer trapped by a game, it is available for the rest of life. When attention is freed, you are living magically because you are free to turn your head this way and that, to move in any direction and to create your own games. The games will no longer be the core, the seed of your life. They will no longer be the pattern from which you unfold.

They will once again be "make believe." But "make believe" will no longer mean "not real." For by "real," what we mean is "of this game." We can switch games and still feel worthwhile. Our feeling of self-worth will not depend on winning one game but on remaining aware and alive.

The game will no longer be our seed but another seed will take its place. This new seed, a pattern coming from that connection to the earth, is called a "vision" among American Indians, a seed implanted in us by the earth. In a sense, it is "our own game"; it comes from within ourselves. And it can only be truly known through its process of unfoldment in our lives.

When creativity flows through the hole at our center, it spins the vision and, as with a gyroscope, a stability is created in our life. That spinning may be termed "enthusiasm." When creativity flows through a vision, there is enthusiasm.

Some systems of knowledge have developed complex systems based on this idea. Chakras are said to be seven holes through which creativity flows and each chakra takes care of one aspect of the vision.

Enthusiasm is the resultant momentum that is created, and it is called *Kundalini* in Yogic systems. It is represented by an uncoiling snake.

It is interesting to note that the practice of "snake staring" (staring for extended periods at a snake's eyes) that is part of the course at my school, is also used to free the attention from games and thus allow this Kundalini energy to uncoil.

In my opinion, working with animals is the purest form of attention exercise.

CHAPTER 14
ENCOUNTER WITH A BIG SEED

On my first expedition to the jungles of Central America, I traveled with a high school student (I was in college). Our aim was to search for reptiles and amphibians and adventure. We met a couple in a jeep one day who picked us up hitchhiking. They brought us to their rice farm and explained that they were revolutionaries. This was in pre-Sandinista Nicaragua.

It was an area of rolling hills covered with patches of farms cut into the thick jungle. The man, about forty, strong and robust, brought us to a clearing and told us that he wanted us to meet his pet. He whistled and, bounding toward us from distant hills, came a huge white Brahma bull. It stopped short just in front of us to check us out. Its huge head must have contained as much volume as my entire body, not to mention the rest of his incredible bulk.

My high school friend was afraid of cows, let alone such a beast as this. But I am a Taurus and have a particular fondness and empathy for bulls.

The bull eyed me and I eyed it. Within that look was a message, a seed. I asked the man if I could play with his pet and though he seemed surprised, he consented.

I walked right over to the bull and told it straight out that I played rough but I would be gentle so as not to make it look bad. The huge white beast pawed the ground and shook its head as if to say, "I'm ready." As I stared into its eyes, I realized that its forehead must be half the size of my bed.

I grabbed its horns and we were locked in mock combat. The bull took a few steps back as if I were pushing it, then it took a few steps forward "as if" it were pushing me. It even flipped me up in the air a few times.

We went on like this for too short a time and then the owner asked me to stop. He was afraid we were getting too rough. I assured him that I would not hurt his bull but he said that's not what worried him.

Principles of Connecting

In any case, it is that initial look bears noting. Something in both our eyes said that we wanted to play and I felt I could trust the bull to play, without it losing its temper. I understood the bull's nature and the bull understood mine, all in a short look. An exchange of mutual respect also took place.

My friend, Dale, later confessed that he felt utter terror as he watched us. That exchange of respect, of friendship did not take place between him and the bull. Fear stood in the way.

In my many years of working with all kinds of animals, I have learned some principles of communication.

The first is respect. Consider that animal to be a fellow being. It may not wear clothes or read the Sunday paper but, in its own way, it is an accomplished creature that wants respect.

One of my pet cats, for example, is very concerned with his dignity. When he comes into the house, his first thought is food, of course, and he walks over to the food bowl. But not to be thought of as a "pig," he walks close enough to it just to see if something is there. If it's empty, he keeps walking, without missing a step, so as not to show his gluttony. When he is very hungry, he may even dash into the house at high speed and then, realizing I am watching, he puts on the skids and walks the last few steps slowly.

Animals are concerned about your attitude toward them. With animals in the wild, there is first a period of sizing up. Each creature, the human and the animal, waits to see how it feels about the other.

The degree to which I can participate in this sizing up depends on the degree of my own self-confidence. When I am completely confident that I can protect myself, then I can look for other possibilities of interaction, such as play. But if I were unsure of myself then I would try to discover only whether the animal wanted to hurt me and if it was capable of doing so.

If I am fully aware of that species' behavior, then I can look more closely at the individual animal's behavior, his own personality.

So the more knowledge I have about both of us, the more we can interact on a personal level. Our interaction becomes more creative in this way. We do not fear each other and basically trust our understanding of each other's intentions. Now, we can feel free to be spontaneous.

That initial look, the seed, has contained within it all this basic information. And I have experienced the same process with many species. In each case, it is as if I were looking at the same animal, a common consciousness looking out through the eyes of a variety of creatures.

Seeds of Trust

I walked into the house of another biology teacher one day and his twelve-foot Burmese python slinked up to me, wrapped around me and started pushing its snout into my face.

The teacher was used to his pet's behavior and I, having many snakes myself, was used to such behavior as well. But all of a sudden, the teacher realized what his pet was doing and asked me whether it was alright with me. I assured him I was used to snakes wrapping themselves around me.

I could imagine another person's reaction, someone not used to snakes. He might consider it an attack. And indeed, if he became frightened, the snake might also become frightened and react poorly.

My understanding of the snake's intent can itself be considered a seed. Each moment, this seed grows into an understanding of its behavior, in this case, of friendliness. The other person's seed would be an incorrect understanding of the snake's intent, which would actually grow into aggressive behavior on the part of the snake. Each of us creates our own reality by planting particular kinds of seeds. If a seed had violence in it, then violence would grow from it. An ideal seed would contain self-awareness, self-confidence and also accurate knowledge.

Imagine the beautiful plants that can grow from an understanding of yourself!

CHAPTER 15
BALANCED ENERGY

If the energy flows out of your body more than it flows in, then you will not be affected by the energy around you. If the energy flows into your body more than it flows out, then the environment will completely control you and you will have no control. "Balanced energy" means keeping these two energies even. It is as if you lifted a refrigerator so it rested only on one bottom corner: When it is balanced this way, it is easy to move and control. It is big and heavy yet, because it is balanced on a pivotal point, this is no problem. The trick is to keep it balanced as you move it so it doesn't fall over.

In the case of energy, it takes a balancing act to keep the two flows of energy even. Otherwise it will just go all the way in one direction or the other and there is no power.

Many people feel that maximum exertion is maximum power. I have a student who has a rounded back near the shoulders. When he punches, he tightens up his neck and back so most of his energy goes into the roundedness rather than out his fist. The more he tenses up and exerts himself, the more he hurts his shoulders and back, but he has no more power. When he punches the bag, he is doing to his back what he wants to do to the bag.

There is a dynamic going on that this student must become aware of as he punches. He can use the "Passive Observer" exercise to watch himself as he punches to see what he is doing on both a physical and emotional level. Once he can see what he is doing, he can compare that with what he is supposed to be doing, and he can become much more efficient (and stop hurting his back).

Obviously, this tensing behavior is the result of some unresolved emotions which have nothing to do with punching a bag effectively.

The unresolved emotions were a cloud over all his life. Through the mechanics of punching, he could find out the origin of the cloud and separate that from his immediate, everyday activities. Without that, he might have become tenser and tenser until he became debilitated for no "legitimate" reason. He was headed all the way to one extreme and, with all his muscular power, he had no real power.

Cycles of Energy

When you are at one end of a process or of any cycle, there is deterioration, that is, a tendency to begin to transform toward the other end of the cycle. There is a deterioration of one aspect into another aspect (the human body, for example, rotting at death and being transformed into earth).

When you are at one extreme of energy flow, it sometimes feels like you are butting your head against a wall.

The yin/yang symbol shows this. Yet within yin there is the eye of yang, and within yang, the eye of yin. This can represent the pivotal point, which is only possible when yin and yang are balanced.

In Push Hands, as we neutralize the partner's force, shifting back and turning, we are at the same time lining ourselves up to be in an advantageous position to push him back. (We can then push him back or neutralize and push at the same time.) The lining up is the eye of yang within yin.

We don't simply retreat forever; the retreating is done only in relationship to sending our energy in on the other side. One side of the cycle is only relevant in relation to the other side. This is balance.

Power from Balance—Internal Energy

Power comes from the relationship between yin and yang, from the quality of that relationship, of that balance. This is internal power. External power would, on the contrary, come from the amount of yang *as opposed* to yin. There is a limit to the amount of yang you may have. But there is no limit to the perfection of the balance between yin and yang.

The pattern of interaction of yin and yang gives us our power. For example, two seeds of equal size have different potentials—the seed of a redwood and that of a bush, let's say. Their genetic pattern gives them different potentials of size.

We can gain control of the quality of the balance between incoming and outgoing energy. This control is "the gatekeeper." First, we must feel it and become aware of it. Secondly, we must balance it and, thirdly, we can experiment with the specific pattern of the interaction. To do this we must become aware of the inner mechanisms of our being that enable us to do these things.

Dynamics of Balance

Such an inner mechanism is the dynamics of attention (the interaction of attention and creativity). We can learn to concentrate strongly through meditation—focussed attention. We can learn to have the attention flow, as in the Form. We can learn to break up the attention into several parts, each following a different happening in the environment (internal or external), and to keep track of several things at once, as in the intricate flows of energy in Push Hands.

We can experiment with the relationship between each of these sub-attentions. Our attention becomes more complex. We can become aware of more going on around and within us.

When we balance the yin/yang energies and are sure that this balance is being maintained, then any disturbances to that balance we can assume to be happenings in the "energy environment." We can only become aware of the energy environment when our own energies are balanced. Awareness comes from balance.

As an example, when somebody says something, you must hear and understand what they say and listen to your own reactions and opinions as well. You must let their words into your heart and let your heart's words come out in return.

Stepping into This World

Now where is this big "refrigerator" to be moved? Where is it that you are trying to move? I am trying to move into the world to enjoy it and also to create healing. There are many blockages, barriers to entering this world. There are angers, resentments, self-righteous attitudes and complaints about others. This prevents me from loving the world around me. It prevents me from having the energy and the enthusiasm to carry on my work. It holds me back from joy and happiness.

I realize that many times, for example, I have not liked or paid attention to a singer's music because I didn't like them as a person.

I once attended the concert of a folksinger whose singing I had convinced myself I didn't like because I thought of the singer in some negative way (though I can't recall why).

When I heard her music at the concert, the beauty of it was so obvious and overpowering that later I listened to one of her albums I had kept from long ago (but never played), in order to reevaluate my opinion. Then I remembered that I had developed this opinion (possibly groundless) at a time when I was quick to judge people. But I actually liked the music even then and had just allowed an indulgence in negative judgements to create a barrier to my appreciation of beauty. Who knows what other beauty I have cut off from myself?

In this case the energy of my opinion had overpowered the beauty of the music and didn't allow it into my heart (until many years later).

It is important to apply the principles of the dynamics of energy in this practical, everyday way, or it becomes just an intellectual exercise.

When we are around others who either absorb too much energy or send out too much, this is harmful to us. It's hard enough trying to reach that balance, without someone who drains our energy or overwhelms us with energy. You can think of such energy as attention. When you are around such people, notice the effect on the balance of energy inside you and try to maintain your balance. Your body-mind will know what to do.

Love and Play

Here is another explanation of the balance of energy: There's love and there's play. Love and play should be in balance. Play may be thought of as yang and love as yin. Think of everything in your life as a form of either love or play.

Love is living from instinct, and identifying with everything you experience. Nothing is separate from you. Play, or playfulness, is making believe that you are separating yourself out from the world around you. Even thinking is play, in this sense. Now, what in your life belongs to love and what to play?

Take a particular feeling you may have and decide to which it belongs. Are you loving the world around you and are you loving yourself (through this feeling)? Or are you trying to distance yourself from it?

In other words, are you complaining about the world or enjoying it? Are you trying to prove yourself to others, to convince them of your worth? Do you not feel your worth as you can feel the sun on your skin or feel the rush of a cold wind?

One day you will feel it—your worth, your power, your connection to this world. Then love will flow as a free energy, as nature herself works, as the wind flows through forest and desert.

Play, the other quality or energy, will be the laughter that results from this connection, a laughter that says, "I see you!" as a child laughs at hide-and-seek. You see the world around you and you see yourself. You begin to discern the world around you, to understand what everything is (in terms of energy, how it feels).

The Naming Game

The play is a naming play. Things are taken away from your environment and then replaced so you can see what it is someone is talking about. When someone points into the environment and says, "Apple," you don't know what they are pointing to at first. But by taking the apple away, you will be shown what is meant. First there is a whole scene and now there is a piece missing from it. That piece, we call "apple."

To create a world is joyful—to create an understanding of it. But soon we learn that only one understanding will do (in the eyes of others). And that understanding isn't always pleasant for us. We learn disappointment.

The joy then loses something. We feel, "Well, this part of the world is nice, but what unpleasantness awaits around the corner?" The sense of play will bring back joy.

Restoring Play

At this point you need to restore your sense of play but it must be done in such a way that you really feel your play will have an influence on your life.

T'ai-chi must show you how most of the world you know, our society and even your mind, was created by such play. It must convince you that the power of play—once the central power of your life (a power which was lost), can be recaptured and put to good use.

You must learn to let go of any human creation, human play, that is controlling your mind. You must learn to discern which play is good for you and which is not. Then you can build your own system of understanding.

There is a constant pressure within you to let go of this weighty structure of knowledge. Yet there is the fear of not being able to function if you do let it go. (The fear of not being able to retrieve it if you let it go.)

Thus, the function of entertainment (a "safe" form of letting go). But watching entertainment is living vicariously.

Some comedians bridge the gap between "entertainment" and "real life" by challenging our structure of behavior and perception. They can be real teachers.

And during dreaming, the seams of the structure of understanding begin to unravel, to relieve some of the pressure.

The weight of your knowledge vs. the need to let go is sometimes like two geologic tectonic plates pushing up against each other. Sometimes there are earthquakes inside you.

At a certain point, the student sees that the love and play are the two basic aspects of his identity and it has been his loss of identity, the forgetting of himself, that is causing his problems. The more he remembers his identity, the more power he has. He is happy. Love and play are close to the surface and balanced.

CHAPTER 16
INNER ATTENTION

When you come upon a group of wild animals you must establish a relationship with them. This does not consist of negotiations or discussions but of the nature of your behavior.

If you look uninterested in them but instead, concentrate on trying to find food on the ground, turning over rocks, etc., you can slowly approach them. But if you stare directly at them, they will be spooked and run away. This is especially true of hoofed animals.

There are living beings within you called "power animals" and your relationship with them is similar. If you act as an animal importer, caging your animals, the animals will be vicious and thrash about their cage. The same is true with the power animals.

Concern yourself more with the "environment" you both live in. Move about them as a fellow creature. Establish yourself in their understanding as someone responsible for their well-being (by feeding and cleaning their cages).

Inner Eyes

Just as you stare at the imported animal and use your attention to develop a relationship with it, there are "inner eyes" with which you direct your attention to or near the power animals to create a relationship.

Were these power animals stuffed, rather than living, your job would be easier. You could merely put them in place and dust them off once in awhile. But then they wouldn't be power animals. They would be stuffed animals.

Many people have stuffed animals within them. How do your animals feel? Are they alive, with a drive and a will of their own? Do you need to reach an accommodation with them or do you basically ignore them? Or have you been ignoring them for so long that you are unaware of them?

If so, then from time to time they will escape from their cages and snap at you and you won't even know what they are. You may just think you are "feeling bad."

How do you know if there has been an escape? You will find yourself about to do something, to say something, to act in some way. And then you will catch yourself and stop, not because it is a harmful thing you wish to do or say, but because it is not in keeping with your usual behavior. The power animal has made a grab for power.

The Gatekeeper

We are each the gatekeeper at the cage door. We turn the gate into a wall when we don't know the skills of opening and closing.

The mind may be yin (open) or yang (closed). The power animal may be yin (resting) or yang (active). The relationship between you may be yin (cooperative) or yang (antagonistic).

To be the gatekeeper, you must stay somewhat apart from the mind and power animals. You must not consider yourself to be thoughts or feelings, as the animal keeper or the animals.

Become the "look of wonder," as the look on a baby's face—total absorption in what it sees, yet with no comprehension. It just looks, as if to say, "What is this?"

Look at what wants to go through the gate. On one side of the gate are the biological organism and the power animals, the spirits living there.

On the other side are the complex agreements with other people—agreements in names of things, knowledge of all kinds—that connect you to your society.

The gatekeeper, therefore, is not your identity in your society. Its dynamics are not those of your society-identity. It is not like the role of "animal keeper" or "kept animal." It is not the biological man or beast. Rather, it is their relationship—trust, mutual respect as understood through the eyes. It is what tempers the struggle of will between the keeper and the kept. It is the central line of the *I Ching* trigram, the fulcrum across which the two ends are balanced.

Remember that the keeper is also the kept. The keeper is kept by his responsibilities to the animal. He is "kept," perhaps, by his boss.

Natural Habitat

When the animal is thrust into its new home (a zoo, for example), it probably does not understand what is going on, or why it has been brought here.

The keeper, of course, can't explain that to the animal. The relationship between the keeper and the animal becomes the animal's stability in life. The routine of feeding, cleaning, etc., creates a new set of centers around which the animal's life and feelings revolve. It also stabilizes the life of the keeper.

Yet this stability is not enough. An animal in a cage, treated mechanically, loses its spirit and is merely a lump of flesh. Modern zoo concepts place animals in a setting as close to their natural surroundings as possible. They fare better emotionally and physically as well. Their wills are allowed to be expressed more freely in a large, natural enclosure. And they breed more readily.

While our own power animals may be calmed by the routines of our daily lives, they need to live in a natural environment as well. They need to express their wills.

The interaction of attention and creativity creates a natural environment for our power animals.

CHAPTER 17
SPIRIT BREATHING

We use spirit breathing to connect the mind and body. Through the Form, we learn that the momentum created by the movements of the body can influence attention, especially when the attention rides the crest of the wave of momentum.

In spirit breathing, we reverse this process, working directly with the dynamics of attention in the Form. For example, the student is taught to circle the attention in a clockwise direction. When breathing out, this movement of attention sinks down into the earth. When breathing in, the circular movement rises up. It is much the same effect as a rotating barber shop pole.

The whole field of attention around the body is made to move in this way as if it were a cylinder, or a screw moving upwards and downwards with the breath, always in a clockwise direction.

The student notices that this has an effect on the flow of momentum in the form. The "momentum of attention" seems to pull on the momentum of the body. The interaction between these two kinds of momentum becomes a central issue of the Form.

Momentum becomes a common medium or a common language for the attention and the body. It is a medium through which the attention and the body can merge. Since momentum is so intricately connected with the earth (gravity), it is a medium through which the individual can be connected to the earth.

Another way of saying this is that the experience of momentum is, in fact, the result of these interactions. There is a momentum to thoughts, will and emotions as well. By working with the momentum dynamics (the "mechanics"), we can learn principles common to all aspects of our being and better understand the relationship of the various parts of ourselves. This opens up a whole new world of perception.

Source of Behavior

The way we function, once perceiving this new world, is the subject of spirit breathing. Some people function mainly from the criteria of thoughts. Their acts are linked to or controlled by thoughts. Other people's acts are controlled by emotions. Or there is a combination of the two.

Spirit breathers' acts are controlled or influenced by the relationship of all parts of their experience to each other and are ruled by the principle of balance. In order to perceive such balance, their attention must be centered in a "place" other than the elements of that balance—a place of stillness at the center. This is the fulcrum point, the point of stillness, emptiness. Only from this vantage point can the balances of the elements of our being be discernible.

So a student learns to become comfortable with emptiness and fosters an "attitude of emptiness" within his movements. This attitude is not an idea, feeling or other such experience, but rather, efficient functioning without internal comment. It is the acceptance of the mind, body and emotions as the nuts and bolts of the flow of attention of the earth, and an allowance of the earth to function through you.

Therefore, when you push someone in Push Hands, there is no competitive feeling but rather an appreciation that this part of the earth (you) is functioning properly. This efficient functioning is not a zombie-like state—quite the contrary. When the flow of attention is no longer bound up in self-conscious manipulation of one's image, there is great joy. Relationships between people are direct, open and warm.

But if the internal mechanics are askew, then any action, including personal relationships, will reflect that.

No Shortcuts to Learning

Perhaps at this point, you have a yearning to achieve this "efficient joy." You may have even read a sentence here or there that made a difference in your life.

Yet, of course, simply reading a book cannot really bring about great changes in life. This book describes many exercises and training techniques that need to be experienced for any real development.

Even the instructional videotapes listed at the back of the book are no substitute for studying with a legitimate T'ai-chi-Ch'uan teacher. Yet they may be helpful if you cannot find a teacher. They may also serve to galvanize what you learn from your teacher, adding a new dimension to his teachings.

If these words make deep sense to you, it is worth making an effort of searching for a teacher. If not now, then when?

Take a look at your life. You have x number of years left on this earth. How will you spend it? How much will you put up with? How much longer will you delay getting your internal dynamics in order? Do you enjoy the turmoil and melodrama of life? Does the pain and sorrow make you feel you are alive, that you are truly human? Are you afraid of letting go of the anger, pain and fear because at least those emotions fill you up? Will you be emotionally hungry when the anger, pain and fear are gone?

Perhaps these are the thoughts going through your mind. I bring this up because if you try to improve your life simply through reading, you may provide a living for me, but your own life may not improve much.

Teachers at all kinds of schools find that eighty-five percent of the students don't last more than a few months. Yet these students can then say, "I tried that and it didn't help me." Many people have told me they studied T'ai-chi several years ago. After further questioning, it turned out that they once dropped into a T'ai-chi class or even just phoned a school.

Efficient functioning means not playing these games. The people mentioned above manipulated their self-image and wound up with nothing.

The Power of Emptiness

There is a great power in our habits, a great momentum which affects our emotions, thinking-mind and attention. When you foster the quiet, empty center, you can feel this momentum tugging at you, calling you to repeat those habits. Yet by remaining centered, you can let go of these habits.

The attitude of emptiness—this empty focal point of attention, becomes a great power in your life and lets you become efficient in allowing joy to blossom.

Among the ancient Hebrews, the innermost chamber of the temple, the most holy place, was completely empty. This is in keeping with what we learn in T'ai-chi.

Yet how many of us are like a guard at the gate of the innermost chamber, fighting off all adversaries to protect the great treasure within. We were never told that there was no gold in the chamber. We spend our lives protecting what we imagine to be great material treasures—even at the cost of our lives or health. If we were to but take a peek into the holy chamber, we would understand that we do not need to battle. Meditation provides such a peek.

Emptiness and Relationships

As you develop this empty center, people around you will notice it. They will fear it. They will try to pull you away from it because, of course, they want the center of your attention to be on them. Your own habits pull you away from your center in the same way.

It is very difficult to continue developing the silent center because you may feel that you are disappointing your friends (and not bending to their will—or to the will of their habits). But that's life.

Will your growth as a human being be tied to innane habits, by the warping and manipulation of joy, either within yourself or by other people? Will you remain forever fixed to the couch? Will the momentum of your attention remain forever fixed to the momentum of your habits?

Healing with Emptiness

This is why connecting your attention to the flow of physical momentum is so important. If successful, it frees the body and attention from the ravages of the thinking-mind and emotions which, in our society, are often tortured. When the momentums of the body and attention become very smooth, calm and flowing, centered around the empty point, they can then reconnect to the mind and emotions, healing them.

They can then reconnect to other people, healing them as well. These other people will have a relationship with you similar to the moon orbiting around the earth. Their need for healing will draw them to the empty center of balance. Yet their habits will propel them away from that center.

This balance of outward and inward forces is necessary. After all, you don't want to mold people into your own image nor do you want to be affected by their habits. In a proper balance, they will be healed without losing their individuality.

Wouldn't it be nice to be among people who are already balanced and internally cleared? This is probably the greatest motivation for a teacher to teach and a healer to heal.

Meanwhile, you can heal your inner community to give that pleasure to the various elements of your being. You are helping to heal the next "lower level" of body-mind.

Now don't you think the next "higher level" is trying to do the same for you?

There is a balance we need to attain, similar to the forces governing the moon and earth. On the one hand, the human mind and human culture vie for our attention. On the other hand, the cycles and dynamics of nature vie for that same attention. Our culture has all but ripped our attention away from nature so that we may become independent. And the result has been nature's destruction.

Can we connect with nature and at the same time remain individualistic? T'ai-chi-Ch'uan is a teaching which allows us to do so. It teaches us balance on the level of the momentum of attention.

SECTION III

Learning T'ai-chi-Ch'uan

CHAPTER 18
THE BEGINNING STUDENT

When I first visited a T'ai-chi school, I knew only that it involved "strange movements." I walked in just as the practice of the Form began and instantly all reference to time and circumstance was erased.

A deep connection was made, a recognition of something that had been missing in my life. The students would ask from time to time whether a foot should be placed here or there, whether the toes should be aimed to the corner or to the side.

It seemed ludicrous at first to be asking such mechanical questions when the whole nature of the movement served to transform the body into a rubbery liquid. I realized that this was a school of true transformation—not through thinking lofty thoughts, or acting like sweetness and light, but by understanding the real mechanics of transformation.

It struck me favorably that in this martial arts system, no one was punching, kicking or grunting. The transformation apparently came first and the fighting later. But my main reaction was a "Yea!" from my gut. Ten minutes after I had walked in, the teacher, Herb Ray, asked me what I thought. I told him I would be doing T'ai-chi for the rest of my life.

Visiting a T'ai-chi School

Now, many years later, I wonder what goes through the minds of visitors to my school. Certainly, many come expecting to see the punches, kicks and grunts. I do not allow visitors to see the fighting classes. So some people walk in, watch for two or three minutes and then walk out, never to be seen again.

I used to allow visitors to the fighting classes and was urged not to by other teachers. I soon realized why. In martial arts schools that prohibit full contact, the students yell, stamp their feet on the ground and grimace fiercely. This is apparently to make up for the illusory nature of their fighting practice.

T'ai-chi practitioners prefer just to hit each other. While the punches are full force, they are not accompanied by shouts, foot stampings or grimaces. So when a visitor sees our fighting, they feel that this is not "real martial arts." And our movements are very fluid so that all our force goes into the punch and kick. This is unlike the fighting movies in which the martial artists perform mechanically. So the fluid fighting does not appear to be "real."

A karate student visited my school to watch a fighting class and as usual, we were hitting each other harder than usual (ego) and practicing flipping the partner down to the floor, jumping up into the air and landing on the chest of the partner with our shoulders, with full body weight. The walls shook from the vibration of our strikes and from being flipped.

Later, the karate student said he had thought he would see full contact and he was disappointed. I asked him to demonstrate his version of full contact on me and he yelled, stamped his foot and grimaced. But his punch landed an inch away from my chest.

After several such episodes, I just closed the fighting classes to visitors. When you are filled with preconceived ideas, it is hard to be open to what you see. I prefer visitors who have no idea what T'ai-chi is, and come out of curiosity. They can then decide to sign up based on what they see.

On the other side, there are people who feel that T'ai-chi fighting consists of sending out chi energy to knock your opponents over, without needing to move at all. These people want to see Walt Disney kung-fu. There are also people who are strictly interested in the health and meditation aspects of T'ai-chi and are uncomfortable seeing any form of aggression.

So now I leave the fighting to their imagination until they are ready for fighting class. But I do show fighting applications of the Form to give them a preview.

Discipline and Bliss

The visitor to a T'ai-chi school faces another problem. In hard-style martial arts schools there is strict discipline, bowing to the teacher, to the Korean flag perhaps, to a photo of the founder of the style, etc. Students are lined up and should they do something wrong, they are punished.

Then there are schools of metaphysics or enlightenment in which starry-eyed people wander about in bliss. But T'ai-chi-Ch'uan doesn't fit in with either of these categories.

Lately there have been attempts at combining these two approaches. These are consciousness centers in which you are berated for being unenlightened and the guest speaker is there to enlighten you.

I attended an American Indian center recently in which an Indian man was to give a concert using native instruments. He decided instead to have a prayer meeting. We were told that this was very serious and that if we wanted to leave, even for a few minutes, we had to ask his permission. Even if we wished to change our leg position as we sat on the floor, we had to ask his permission.

The prayer meeting turned out to be a complaining session for all the ills in the world and in the participants' lives. It became very negative. Then the leader began chanting in New Age cliches. When he started praying to Jesus, I really got confused.

I cringe when I hear even one New Age cliché, but after fifty or so I had to use all my meditative powers to remain relaxed. The session lasted an hour-and-a-half beyond its allotted time and that was fine. We shouldn't be so regulated by time.

I kept saying to myself, though, that I should just get up and leave, but I didn't want to disturb the others. When the leader asked everyone to get up and stretch, I spoke to the owner of the center and told her I was leaving.

The next day an irate participant called me and complained that I hadn't asked the leader's permission to leave. Apparently you could not leave unless you went through a special ceremony. If I had been told that I couldn't leave unless I went through his ceremony, I would have used a favorite expression of one of my students, "Watch me!" I believe in respecting others but in this case I felt the routine was going too far. When it got to the point where the owner of the center said that we were all living in darkness and this fellow was going to save our souls, I felt that my own respect had been stepped on.

No Hype

The problem with attracting large numbers of students to a T'ai-chi school is that it has no shenanigans. It has the romantic value of your corner vegetable stand. The T'ai-chi folks are just like your neighbors (and often *are* your neighbors). So there's no hype to latch onto when you first arrive as a visitor.

In my opinion, many people who seek some sort of "enlightenment" are really seeking a pattern of opinions or a persona to hide behind. They may have inner pain or dissatisfaction and feel that if they have the "correct" beliefs, smile a lot or are berated on a regular basis, all will be solved. Whatever their real problem, it seems too painful to deal with directly.

But in T'ai-chi, the "oh, poor suffering me" routine is considered just that—a routine. The macho stance is also a routine, a rigid pattern of behavior designed to hide oneself away.

I believe that it is only those people who are willing to directly face their "routines" and let them go, who are attracted to T'ai-chi. They realize that it is the routines themselves that are the problem. The T'ai-chi Form hints of "no routines," just fluidity.

Giving up such routines is not always comfortable—in fact, it can be extremely uncomfortable. It is like the feeling of falling in a dream, where you're out of control. You tense up to stop the fall, but it's as if the floor has been pulled out from under you. You're grabbing for something to hold on to—just as people try to hold on to their habits. When you give up a routine, it seems as if you've given up something important, so you feel empty or depleted. Life itself has an empty space. It can even make you physically ill.

You can go through your whole life making up "fashioned creatures" and playing games—or you can simply "let go." You may have to be uncomfortable for awhile, but then you can live an enjoyable life!

Jumping Off the Cliff

There is another problem for the beginning student. Most people have a psychological wall of protection around them, a physical, psychological and emotional space which no one may enter. This protected space is so much a part of our lives that we hardly notice it, except when we allow a lover into that space (if we ever do). That is one appeal of a relationship—that finally, someone has entered your precious space.

But the confidence and self-awareness developed through T'ai-chi practice allow us to drop that protection to a large extent. We learn, in Push Hands, to allow our partner's energy to flow into our space and then we deal with it inside us.

This presents a visitor with the psychological equivalent of standing at the edge of a cliff. There is a big, open space in front of them and, even if they don't jump, they may get dizzy just standing there.

The cliff is the seasoned students' relative lack of a protected space. It is that they act and speak spontaneously rather than calculating their actions. This freedom and openness often causes fear in others, fear covered up with ridicule or anger or hate.

And then there is the teacher. He is most likely called by his first name. The students don't bow to him but just walk up and say, "How's it going?" There are no colored belts to even let you know who the teacher is. And how would you know a good teacher from a poor one with a system so different from the movies?

Finding a Good Teacher

These are my suggestions for determining a good teacher and school:

1. The teacher should be familiar with and be able to teach all aspects of T'ai-chi including the Form, Push Hands, fighting, an elemental system (the elements), Taoist philosophy, some form of healing (acupuncture, acupressure or herbal medicine), some form of Chi-gung or spirit breathing, and camping or some way of participating in nature—the shamanic aspect of T'ai-chi.
2. The teacher should be willing to explain things to the student and answer questions.
3. The teacher should watch the students carefully and continually make corrections.
4. The teacher should be in decent physical shape.
5. The school should have a relaxed atmosphere so you feel relaxed yourself.

6. The students should be eager to help you.
7. If the teacher has had a background in karate, he should have studied more than a year of T'ai-chi for each year of karate. This is because it takes at least a year of T'ai-chi to break the habits of each year of karate training. You should find out if he is teaching pure T'ai-chi or some mixture.
8. There should be no belt systems.
9. The teacher should look you right in the eyes while talking to you and those eyes should be clear and relaxed.
10. You should not be pushed into joining the school.
11. The teacher should explain his pricing policy and how and what he teaches.
12. Seeing him practice the Form should relax you.

There are a lot of "shoulds" here, but I think they are all sound.

It is difficult for a newcomer to distinguish a "legitimate" T'ai-chi teacher from someone who took a short course and then became a "master." In the martial arts world today there is a lot of discussion about how the "weekend warrior" teachers have injured the quality of martial arts and have caused people to lose interest.

To be fair, there is nothing wrong with someone, who has learned a little of a discipline, teaching others to expose them to the discipline. But he should make his own background and level of competence clear. I would love to see people of all levels practicing the Form in parks together as they do in China.

And who is to be appointed to judge the competence of another? The point some teachers make is that inexperienced people are setting themselves up as masters and this confuses the students. Or, they mix karate with T'ai-chi and tell the students they are learning pure T'ai-chi.

So the newcomer should visit several schools, if possible, to get a broad view. Finally, something in the newcomer's mind must click and he will know this or that school is the right one.

I receive calls all the time in which I get the third degree from a potential student. I certainly don't mind. Rather, I appreciate that this person took the trouble to compile a list of questions and I answer them happily.

Creating Reality

Sometimes a caller challenges the "power" of T'ai-chi-Ch'uan. "Can T'ai-chi beat karate?" is the typical question. The question is put in a challenging tone.

I merely explain the advantages and disadvantages of each and suggest that the caller decide what he really wants in a martial art. When the caller realizes that I have not responded in a defensive way but rather in an informative way, he becomes respectful and his tone completely changes.

This is called "creating reality." I respond to him as if he has been respectful and he becomes respectful. This is because many people know themselves only through the reaction of other people to them. They may not (usually do not) realize that the behavior of other people is in response to their own behavior.

Yet their own behavior is regulated to a large degree by the responses of others to them. If I treat someone who is obnoxious and threatening "as if" they are being gentle and respectful, they may believe that, in fact, they are being respectful. Their behavior will often change to correspond to that self-image.

This is a key secret in dealing with other people. Their behavior is regulated by their self-image and their self-image is shaped by the reaction of others to them. The advertising industry knows this very well.

This is really saying the same thing as the Middle Eastern story about the two men sitting outside an ancient city, talking to two travelers (mentioned earlier).

Investigate Your Own Motives

Before investigating T'ai-chi schools and teachers, investigate yourself. What are the reasons you want to learn T'ai-chi? What do you hope to get from it?

If you say, for example, that you want more harmony in your life, perhaps between the mind and body, ask yourself why you feel you are not harmonious now? What deficiencies have you found within yourself that you wish to correct?

Or are you just in love with those movements and you'd like to flow like water? Or are you tense and have aches and pains and worry a lot? Do you feel you need help to just enjoy your life? Are you interested in physically or emotionally defending yourself?

In any case, examine your motives. This will make it easier for you to choose the right school.

Attitudes Toward Learning

The cynic says, "Why should I have to pay the teacher? I deserve to be taught for free. Who does he think he is?" You pay the teacher to keep him alive so he can keep teaching you.

I always had a problem learning anything from anybody. I would spend years studying with a teacher, but resisted the teaching the whole way. This was because those very habits and tensions the teacher was trying to eliminate, I cherished dearly. They were part of me and I felt that a threat to my habits was a threat to me. My attitude was "I dare you to teach me!"

The teachings themselves gradually sunk into me and I realized the absurdity of my attitude. How could I expect the teacher to do a good job teaching me when I resisted his teaching?

I also realized that I probably will have reservations about any teacher I study with. If I were to wait for a "perfect" human to teach me, I would be waiting a long time. I had to accept the valuable teaching of the teacher even though I recognized (or thought I did) some negative qualities in him as well.

Our delicate sensitivities and opinions of others often keep knowledge from us. Few people want to give up their tension. Tension is the army of the mind. Once the mind realizes that T'ai-chi requires it give up its army and redistribute some of its power to the body-mind, the mind tries to stop you from practicing. You find any excuse not to practice. Complaining about the teacher can be one of those excuses.

Being a Parent to the Inner Child

It is essential that the beginning student realize that the thinking-mind is like a little child being asked to give up its toys. It is a living being. It will resist any inroads to its power.

Allow the mind to come up with its excuses to avoid practicing. But practice anyway. The mind will plead its case. You can listen, smile and even nod, but practice anyway. This teaches you to decide to practice from your will. Your will will direct your behavior more and more. This is not the will of the thinking-mind. It is the same kind of will that a plant has to grow, that the sun has to rotate on its axis. It is the expression of nature channeled through the tan-tien.

The more power your will gains, the more clever the mind becomes in trying to get you to give up your practice. Its reasoning will become very convincing. If you remain centered in your will, it becomes a key to unlock the power of the mind. The will is like a fire being fed by air (the mind). It grows hotter and hotter.

The Form is like the furnace that contains this hot fire and channels it to do useful work. In a furnace, you can melt ore to create pure metal. The Form allows you to melt your habits and tensions to become a pure human.

Uncontrolled fire can be harmful. Likewise, a battle between the mind and will can be harmful unless it is done within the context of a discipline of harmony.

This can be a very lighthearted practice, as when you laugh at the antics of a child. Yet it is serious because it deals with the very nature of your being. While you may laugh inwardly at the antics of a child, you realize that you must consider how to respond to him carefully so as to bring him up well.

The T'ai-chi student faces a similar situation. He becomes a parent to his own child and thus places the body-mind at its rightful position of parent to the mind. This also has a beneficial effect on his relationship to his own human parents because he can then appreciate what they had to put up with in bringing him up.

Centering Your Kite

It is expressed this way: The will is located at the center, the tan-tien, while the thinking-mind is located at the extremes. While the mind may wave in the wind like a beautifully colored kite, it must be attached to the center (the person holding the kite string). Otherwise it will blow away.

The beginning student is learning to hold onto the kite string while the kite is being blown about by strong winds. It is serious business but it is also fun.

In several cultures, kite-flying is considered a sacred practice because of its metaphoric value.

Sore Legs

The beginning student also faces a considerable physical problem. The full weight of the body must sink into the legs. The average person straightens out the knees so that the weight sinks through the leg bones. This does not allow for fluidity.

Beginning students' legs shake and wobble until the muscles gain the strength to hold up the body. Bent knees and spring-like muscles result in a resilient body.

When the teacher tells the students to hold their positions so he can check each person's posture, the class can become torturous, depending on the number of students. As soon as the teacher's back is turned, you will see knees suddenly straightening out.

I advise the students to expect sore legs twenty-four hours a day for at least two months. To build leg strength, you can stand on one leg with the other resting on a raised object (three or four feet above the ground). Allow the standing leg to hurt for ten seconds and then switch legs. Keep the knees bent and the back fairly straight.

One-leg squats are also helpful, keeping the raised leg stretched out in front. You can hold on to a chair (or a pole) at first until your legs strengthen.

Another important exercise helps to develop the "crease" between the thigh and hip. This crease allows you to really sink into your root.

Place two small beach balls (ten to twelve inches in diameter), one in each crease. Lean forward until the ball is squeezed between the lower abdomen and the upper thigh. Walk around in this squatted position. You can also try walking up stairs like this. Be prepared for sore legs.

To develop balance, stand on the two beach balls, one foot on each ball. You can also play Push Hands with the front or rear leg on a beach ball. The ball can also be used to push your partner so he can develop the ability to turn and neutralize. You try to keep the ball pressed directly into his chest as you hold it between your hands.

For the beginning student, the beach ball is most often used to relax the back and chest. You lie on the beach ball (on your back or chest) and move the ball in increments, up and down under the body. This will loosen the muscles and the spine, but in a soft way that will not damage anything. A dollar beach ball goes a long way.

All Together Now

A serious problem faced by the T'ai-chi initiate is to get all the parts of himself doing the same thing at the same time. His shoulders often turn without the waist. Or the head will turn to look ahead to the spot where he will step, before the body is finished with the previous move. Meanwhile, his mind is thinking about his girlfriend. "His works lie scattered," as the Gnostics would say.

The teacher must shift various parts of the body around so that they are all doing the same thing. More importantly, he continually asks, "Where is your attention? Is it on thinking a thought? Is it on a part of the body? Is it on your senses? It should be centered at the center, the tan-tien."

Centering the Attention

Unless the attention is kept centered, it cannot grow. Part of our development as humans is to nourish and exercise the attention so that it can grow by expanding and connecting with other "centers of attention." The individual's attention "hub" is the body-mind and its "spokes" grow out to other "hubs." But if your own attention is not centered, it cannot grow in this manner and is always lonely for the center. You can be in a crowd and still be lonely if the attention is not in the "staircase of body-minds." Each floor is like another level or kind of body-mind. If you stand in the center of any level, you can see all the way up and down the staircase.

If your attention is not centered in the body-mind, you can't really connect with others, except verbally and visually.

So the attention of the beginning student must be centered in order for it to grow and connect. The student's eyes must look straight ahead from the body, turning with the body and not darting about.

The eyes become like pools of water at the bottom of a waterfall. The falling water is the senses and body-mind is the bedrock below. Sights, flowing through the eyes, land on the body-mind at the tan-tien.

In this way the eyes not only perceive light, but also another kind of energy that is felt in the pit of the belly. As the student flows through the physical space around him, this energy flows through him. The boundaries of his body, the space surrounding it and the energies flowing through it are no longer felt as separate things, and the entirety of his experience is perceived as part of his flesh. His nervous system seems to grow into the environment. The Form becomes a living internal presence, its grounded, flowing quality a guide to the missing links between the forgotten parts of your true flesh and the forgotten creator of that flesh.

Teaching the Beginning Student

A teacher must keep this in mind at all stages of a student's progress. The principles and practices he lays down at the beginning must be solid enough to build upon.

This is why a legitimate teacher is one who has gone through all the stages of training at least to some extent. Otherwise, even his ability to teach the Form will suffer.

And each student is different, requiring a different emphasis, different ways of explaining things. Each year, each day, the same student is different and needs to hear different advice. The teacher is aware of the tremendous variations in his student and plays a balancing act of what to say, depending on the student's needs.

His own actions and behavior are used to affect the students' patterns of attention, to aid in teaching. I illustrate this in fighting class. I punch a student in the belly while he tries to neutralize with his elbows. Before each punch, I tell the student whether he will successfully neutralize or not. Yet each punch is exactly like the next.

I "know" whether he will neutralize or not because we can freeze the partner's attention. We reach into the partner and manipulate the attention. I either freeze his attention or not. This is to illustrate that T'ai-chi has a great deal to do with developing skills of attention.

Being Picky about the Simple Basics

Students will often accuse the teacher of being "picky" when he adjusts the palm or the posture only half an inch. Yet the student can tell that when this minor adjustment is made, it "feels right" (usually meaning there is more pain in the legs). When the student advances, that half inch will mean the difference between energy flowing through the body or being cut off. There is no room for sloppiness.

Sometimes a student will come to me from another teacher. Since he has already learned the Form, he expects to begin in my school with Push Hands. I once agreed to this even though it was obvious that I could not build upon the student's weak foundation. It became extremely difficult for this student to progress until he finally agreed to work on his Form. I felt I had done him a disservice by not insisting that he learn the Form over again. He could have saved at least two years of struggle.

I have found that continual work on the simplest, beginning exercises is very important throughout one's progress. The mind may taunt me, questioning why I'm wasting my time on such simple stuff. But I know that without those basics, my T'ai-chi would deteriorate.

The following exercise is one I enjoy a great deal. I may "give the reins" to my body, "allowing it" freedom of movement. It may go into very pleasing, repetitive movements for long periods of time. Then it may go into a stretching routine, making up stretches I've never seen before. I marvel at its intelligence and at the pleasurable feelings its motions generate.

Slowly, the attention shifts and the person who is at the helm is no longer that separate observer. It is the body itself. The observer can see the mechanism causing the body to move in such ways. In fact, it *is* that mechanism. And that observer goes about its business as "I" would go about adding up a series of numbers.

From that vantage point, awareness of the body's kinesthetic needs, dreaming dynamics, energy flow, etc., are as obvious as shapes and colors, the ordinary physical world, is to "me." This vantage point knows its own needs, has access to its own teachers and can heal as easily as I can count simple numbers.

When a T'ai-chi teacher teaches the basics, he has this more advanced purpose in mind. He tries to see within the student to his inner vantage point, and teach in such a way as to point it out to the student. He sees the student's awkwardness as an unwillingness to sink his attention to the inner vantage point, and cajoles, tricks and pushes the student to let go of his desperate grip on the vantage point we are all familiar with.

Each of those half-inch adjustments is like removing a finger from the student's grip. In this analogy, the student stands on the cliff of his mind and jumps into the valley of body-mind. The teacher must constantly assess how close to the edge the student has moved and how strong are his wings (the skill of working with energy flow).

Dealing with Different Kinds of Students

While it is true that many of the students simply want to learn martial arts, it is impossible to learn an internal martial art without going through these internal transformations.

I phrase the inner aspects of T'ai-chi-Ch'uan as the dynamics of attention, to complement the body dynamics. This is an easy pill for people to swallow but allows me to "tamper" with the student's attention, to unravel all the knots.

I can then explain how adjustments in the dynamics of attention affect the student's everyday life. After awhile, I can begin to use less mechanical terminology and speak in shamanistic terms, explaining that the earth is a living creature, gravity is the attention of the earth, etc.

This is also important for the T'ai-chi students who are a bit "glassy-eyed," wanting to travel to other planes and know who they were in their past lives.

A friend of mine told me that when she was with me she felt her feet had sunk beneath the earth. "Oh, you feel good?" I asked. "No, I feel terrible." I said, "When I'm with you I feel like I'm floating in the clouds." "Oh, you feel good?" she asked. "No, I feel terrible," I replied. Teaching T'ai-chi from the viewpoint of mechanics grounds the student.

A big difficulty for students who are mainly interested in self-defense is patience. It takes about a year to start fighting class. I solve this by showing fighting applications of the Form and by conducting a weekly kung-fu exercise class. Movements from the animal forms (snake, tiger, mantis, monkey, crane and drunken styles) are repeated twenty-five to fifty times each and the fighting applications are shown. This gives a taste of things to come and helps develop strength, balance and flexibility.

Seeing the Inner Forest

But there is a deeper problem than patience, one that goes to the root of our seeming helplessness. Students complain that there is a resistance to practicing and to coming to class. The challenge to the mind's power causes this.

The student must have a tool that will keep him practicing (by centering on the will), unlock the mind's secrets, teach him to change vantage points of attention, and also develop "inner eyes" that will enable him to see the forces controlling his life.

A student complains how hard it is for him to stick with T'ai-chi but how much he wants to. I tell him that when he is again faced with wanting to do the Form and finds a resistance, to feel the parts of himself that are pulling him each way. Don't get involved in the rational arguments pro or con. Simply feel the tug towards and the tug away from practicing or from coming to class.

Get to know these tugs, for they are like living beings, lurking in a forest. They are hard to see because they are camouflaged and blend in with their surroundings.

Get to know the pulls on your emotions, on your energy, on your attention, as you would get to know the animals in a forest. You must learn the appearance of the animal, its behavior, its life cycle. Then you will become familiar with the forest and the relationship between its plants, animals, soil, air, water, weather, etc. It will start to make sense to you, just as if you were watching a nature show on television.

Get to know the inner forest in the same way. There are beings in you and they have an effect on your life. In the beginning, they just run rampant and you bump into them because you can't see them. Then you complain.

Rather than complaining, look and observe. See the beings within you with no judgement for or against them. Take responsibility for your "inner" world.

And after all, that is the greatest fear in T'ai-chi. If you can really see what's going on, if you can really take control of your life, then you are responsible for your failure or success. And you can't blame anyone else.

The Awkward Beginner

The beginning student wants to know, "Am I the only one who feels clumsy?" You might be an athlete. You may have studied karate for many years. But you will still feel clumsy when you begin T'ai-chi.

Students from a karate school once came to my school to get a taste of T'ai-chi. They would work out three times a week, pushing themselves to the limit, working up a sweat in their karate school. After practicing the beginning exercise with us, they commented that this was the most difficult "workout" they had ever had. We were doing only slow, smooth movements, with slow breathing. But they had never practiced sustained positions with slow breathing and sustained concentration. This kind of "exercise" called on resources and abilities they had not developed.

Each joint, muscle and nerve must be retrained for maximum efficiency. The oxygenating system of the body—heart, lungs and blood—are developed to get more oxygen per breath. The muscle fibers must grow in a different way to develop tensile as well as compression strength, so they won't tear. The attention must be exercised as if it were composed of muscles.

Everyone feels awkward at first. The task before you seems enormous and unending. One of my students says that it doesn't pay to learn anything in T'ai-chi because as soon as you learn it, the teacher gives you something else to learn. It never ends.

But you have one great advantage. T'ai-chi works the way the body works. It simply develops your innate abilities rather than teaching you to counteract your physical and psychological makeup. It gives you back to yourself. That is why such disciplines as Zen and T'ai-chi are called "selling water by the river." You are teaching the student something he already knows (but forgot).

For example, the body is composed of more than two-thirds water. Most of the body is in the state of "colloidal suspension," a gel. If you poke gelatin, it responds easily yet remains firm. T'ai-chi teaches you how to use your gel nature to maximum efficiency.

Training the Attention

When students get frustrated at their awkwardness, this really means that it is hard for them to concentrate on what they're doing. Whenever you are completely immersed in a project, your concentration is completely connected to the project and time seems to fly by. I'm often surprised at what time it is after writing or editing videos.

The more you concentrate, the easier it is. Attention is the lubrication that makes your work go smoothly. It is the medium through which energy flows.

If you train the attention, your progress will improve. Catching flies on the wing is an example of a good exercise. When I worked in the Bronx Zoo, I had to catch bats in a cage. Since they use sonar, bats can evade any obstacle, so my hands had to be faster than their reactions.

Many years ago, I studied the behavior of frogs in a Nicaraguan bamboo forest. They had to be located by sound rather than by sight. It was night and the jungle was dark. (The frogs did not come out on bright, moonlit nights.) If the flashlight were to be turned on, they would stop singing and would be impossible to find. So I had to distinguish an individual frog peeping from among thousands in the area. The problem was made more difficult because they only peeped for a few seconds and then stopped.

It got so that my attention to their songs became like a solid cord connecting me to the frog. After each set of peeps (or croaks), I moved a bit closer to the sound. When I felt very close to it, I shone my flashlight on the spot, caught, marked and recorded the frog's position.

This type of exercise solidifies the attention so that it seems as physical as a rock. Imagine the difference in the lives of people who have never developed their attention as compared to those who make a specialty of it. The world is fuller for those who can pay attention.

Practical Attention Exercises

A more practical exercise for most people is to concentrate on a single instrument while listening to an orchestra. Then listen to the same piece again, concentrating on a different instrument.

Or, find two songs with a similar beat and play one near each ear. Try to allow each song its independence (divide your attention into two parts and allow each to follow one of the songs). In some songs on the early "Queen" albums, each of the four instruments play fairly independent tunes and you must find their common union inside your head.

These exercises develop the ability to concentrate on several things at once. This is important in coordinating the movements of each part of the body.

The key idea here is that if you develop the mechanics of attention, you can then "attach" the attention to any particular thing (body parts, ideas, sensory information, etc.). The skill you gain in the dynamics of attention can be applied to any particular area of your life.

While standing, concentrate on an object a few feet away on the ground. Place both index fingers in front of your head, touching each other. Slowly move the fingers to the sides and then back again, following them with your peripheral vision. But keep your eyes fixed on the object on the ground.

Then, starting in the same position, move your fingers down, outward and then up, inward and down to the original position, again following only with your peripheral vision.

Next, do the same exercises but with eyes closed and follow the fingers with your inner attention. This will unlock the attention from your usual senses and allow it to flow along different pathways. This will help when you learn to fill your body and your surroundings with attention.

Developing these pathways of attention is like putting a large drop of water on a slanted piece of wood. At first, the drop remains where it is due to whatever physical force resists its flowing down the incline. But if you wet your finger and create a pathway of moisture on the wood and then connect it to the drop, that drop will flow exactly along the path you created. You eliminated much of the resistance along a particular path. The same can be done with attention.

Next, you can learn to recombine parts of your attention you originally separated. You might poetically say that each part of the attention was sent out like the roots of a plant, to absorb nutrients from your environment. Recombining the attention is like bringing the nutrients back.

There are stereo photos in magazines about electron microscopy. The microscopes take the stereo photos of cells, nuclei and other very tiny objects. Two photos are presented on the page. You must use one eye to see each of the two photos and then, inside your head, recombine the photos into a third photo. You will see this third photo on the page even though it is not really physically there. It is in your mind. That third photo is three-dimensional.

This is the process you go through when looking out at the world. The images in your eyes are flat. They are spots of light on your retina. You combine them in your head to create the three-dimensional world. This is the same process as combining two ideas and coming up with a third, a process we usually call creativity. It is like the male and female producing a baby.

In another exercise, you place your finger on various parts of the body and press. Concentrate on the pressure. This will help fill your body with attention.

Play a wind instrument (a cheap wood flute will do), sustaining a single note with each full breath. Try to open the windpipe so that the vibration in the flute vibrates the air in your lungs. Allow the lungs and flute to join through their mutual vibration. This will give you a feeling for how all your individual parts will join through the vibration of energy in the attention.

Meditation

It is also important to allow the attention to come to rest on a regular basis. Sit in a comfortable position (lying down may lead to sleep) with no visual or auditory distractions. Concentrate on something physical, such as your breathing, allowing the breath to move slowly in and out.

If thoughts come, allow them their freedom but do not follow them or try to stop them. Just remain concentrated on the breath. You may use a timer if you need to end the session at a certain time. Or, you may light a candle or incense and end when it burns down to the bottom.

You can place a low candle two feet in front of you while seated on the floor (back straight but relaxed), and keep the palms up. Concentrate a foot past the flame and breathe slowly and smoothly. You are now creating (or rather, allowing) a flow of attention from the eyes, to the spot you are concentrating on, back through the candle, into the belly (using diaphragmatic, belly breathing) and back up to the eyes.

Meditation empties the patterns in the attention since it is done in a dim, quiet place. I find that doing sitting meditation in an attic with dried, old wood beams serves the purpose well. The wood seems to "absorb" all the patterns in the attention.

When the attention is thus calmed, any pattern impinging on the attention stands out more. We are so inundated with noises, bright lights and television that the subtler perceptions get lost. Sitting meditation allows such perceptions as the biological workings of the body to become noticeable.

Another subtle perception that is important in T'ai-chi is the pattern of attention in another person. If your own attention is crowded with flashy patterns, it will be hard for you to notice another person's attention patterns.

Paying Attention

The beginning student is taught to notice the inconsequential. You will find that whatever you pay attention to is no longer inconsequential because it becomes part of your life. Your life will become fuller, your attention sharper.

Many opportunities are lost in life due to overlooking things we thought unimportant—a casual remark that could lead you to a business opportunity, a furtive glance, etc. Don't worry that you'll fill your brain with information too quickly. We normally use very little of our brains anyway. There's plenty of empty space in there.

After you practice this exercise for a month or two, people may notice that your eyes appear different. They may look more connected to your soul. This is because when you look, you really notice. You allow the world around you to flow into you. And when you look at another person, you allow their attention to flow into you.

This attention is no longer perceived as a threat, as a penetration of your individuality. Through these exercises, you realize that attention is a universal energy like gravity. You no longer protect it as if you had only a little bit of it. You "bathe" in the vast quantity of attention that fills the world.

And then you realize a strange truth. That which you coveted, which you hoarded, is all around you. Coveting only serves to disconnect you from what is freely available.

Suggestions for Practicing the Form

At the beginning, it is difficult to remember all the details of the Form. I suggest that before commencing, decide what you will concentrate on—the mechanics, the weight distribution, breathing, fluidity, rooting, compression and expansion, flow of attention, etc. You can even practice just the shifting and stepping, and leave the arms at the sides.

Allow the other aspects of the Form to suffer for the moment. Trust that each time you practice for a specific purpose, you will add to your overall skill.

Then concentrate on two things at a time, mechanics and rooting, or looking straight ahead and using the hips, etc. When you have practiced and feel comfortable with every possible combination, do three at a time, and so forth.

You can then practice just one movement over and over again, combining all aspects. Meanwhile, continue to practice the Form straight through at other times. The skills gained in one movement will carry through to the whole Form.

The next exercise serves to stamp the Form into your mind and body. "Practice" the Form in your mind while sitting, unmoving. Breathe according to the proper breathing for the Form, but do the movements only in your internal visual imagery. This will connect the pattern of the Form to your imagination.

You may find that even though it is easy to practice the Form physically, it is very hard to do mentally. You may have competing mental patterns vying for attention. When the mental pattern and the physical pattern unite, you have begun to unite mind and body.

Practice Habits

Should you forget portions of the Form when you are just starting out, don't worry. Do the portions you know and make up the rest. You may think that this will result in remembering the wrong movements. Look at it this way. As you learn more, finer details of the Form will be taught to you. Or, you may think you have been doing the Form correctly, but as these finer details are shown to you, you realize that you were glossing over them.

At the beginning you may make up some movements that resemble what you think you learned, so long as the flow and the feeling of it are in keeping with T'ai-chi principles. No matter how far off the mark your movements turn out to be, they will probably not be any further off the mark than your mechanically correct movements are from "perfection." Furthermore, the quality of movement, the feel of it, is even more important than the particular kind of movement. After all, there are several styles of T'ai-chi with differing movements, yet they are all considered to be "proper."

There are also videotapes available to help you practice at home so that you need never forget what you learned (see the last pages of this book for details).

The students who progress rapidly are not necessarily the ones with the greatest natural talent. They are the ones who practice regularly and show up in class regularly. They are self-motivated, don't give in to excuses not to practice and are open and accepting of instruction. They trust the teacher's competence.

Trusting the Teacher

This last issue was brought home to me when I invited my students to some ceremonies in the Druid (Celtic) and American Indian traditions. They attended and enjoyed the ceremonies. At one point, I realized how strange these practices must seem to people who only recently even thought of getting involved in anything outside of the "mainstream culture." I remarked on this to the leader of the Druid ceremony and he explained to me that the students trusted me. They trusted that if I recommended something to them, it must be beneficial.

Although it seems obvious, I had never thought of it that way before, and I appreciated that I was the recipient of such trust. It is only the integrity of one's teachings, I believe, that can inspire trust. This means that what you teach in T'ai-chi must come from the heart, from your own life experience, and not just from repeating what you read in a book or see in a kung-fu movie. And that means devoting your whole life to what you do.

I was once speaking to a T'ai-chi master whom I had just met and he asked me if I had ever experienced any of what I wrote in *Movements of Magic*. The question astounded me. Did he think I would write all that out of my imagination? Teaching from the heart means teaching what you are experiencing, what you are living. How could I teach something that I did not really understand or experience? Unfortunately, the above-mentioned T'ai-chi-Ch'uan master confided in me that he did just that. I made no comment in return, as I was stunned.

Trust Yourself

There is a tendency to revere a teacher too much and believe that if you do everything he or she does, exactly as he does it, with no input or questioning on your part, then you will magically achieve whatever it is you want to achieve. This isn't real respect. It is just laziness.

The student should question and experiment from day one. Otherwise T'ai-chi will not be alive inside you. You will know its appearance but not its substance.

So if you forget a move, feel free to make one up until you go back to class and can be corrected. The Taoist Gods won't strike you dead. And if the teacher is angered by your made-up moves, just say, "Hey! Lighten up!" (If the Taoist Gods are angered, just tell them, "Bob Klein told me to do it," and I'll handle them.)

CHAPTER 19
THE INTERMEDIATE STUDENT

When you're the new kid on the block during your first few lessons, you may feel self-conscious watching the more advanced students. You may feel that you're imposing on those students when you ask them for help.

But you are actually performing valuable services for the more experienced students. First of all, it is hard to judge your own progress in T'ai-chi. You tend to make the same mistakes over and over again especially when inefficient patterns of behavior have been programmed into you since birth. At my school, we are currently studying how many times I have to tell a student something before he corrects it in his practice. Some say one thousand. Others say ten thousand. That will give you an idea of the range of possibilities. Progress is slow and gradual, so it's hard to tell.

But when a fresh, innocent new student comes to the school, the intermediate or advanced student can see "where he's been." And he can remember that he, too, was once awkward and stiff. This will allow him to feel better about himself because at least he's better than you!

Another benefit for the experienced student is that teaching is the best form of learning. When the beginner student asks, "Which direction should my foot be facing?" the instructor needs to know or find out the answer.

This is why most T'ai-chi-Ch'uan masters teach all the classes, even the classes for beginners. Otherwise, the basic foundation of the master's own abilities will become sloppy. The intermediate student learns as much from teaching as he does from his own studies.

"Winning" Turns into "Unifying"

Cooperation is the basic atmosphere in a T'ai-chi school. Everyone helps each other out and cheers each other on. Yet some T'ai-chi practices naturally bring up feelings of competition. Push Hands takes advantage of this transitional period in a student's life. The intermediate student is filled with a cooperative feeling from Form classes, and now begins a practice in which you try to push your partner off balance and prevent him from doing the same to you.

Yet if you operate from the perspective of competition, you will lose the game. Push Hands requires a melding, a union. This creates a basic foundation. The moment you tense up to prepare to push, you get pushed by your partner. All the little behaviors associated with gearing your effort to win (tensing up, raising your shoulders, etc.) actually make you susceptible to losing. The push must come out in the same manner that a seedling grows. Seedlings do not gird themselves to grow. Growth is a natural process. The push must grow from Push Hands in the same manner. And a little seedling can push its way through concrete.

It is very frustrating to have to give up the desire to win in order to win. When the push comes from a natural, spontaneous, simple movement, the mind can't take credit for it. You must do less to achieve more—less extraneous movements associated with the idea of winning. Push Hands is a study in frustration.

Making Statements

When the student girds himself to push, we say he is "making a statement" or "telegraphing" his intentions. Much of our behaviors consist of making such statements. It is our way of saying who we are. If we can perceive the underlying statements another person is making as they interact with us, we can discover the motivation for their behavior.

On the other hand, if we can eliminate such covert making of statements in our own behavior, our lives will become more simplified. In this latter way of living, your words, actions and intentions are one. Your actions are honest. Your words are honest. You are not using a conversation to establish your identity in the mind of another person but rather to convey information or to enjoy the other person's company.

Much of our aggravation with other people comes from their inability (or unwillingness) to allow your covert "statements" about your identity to affect their actual impression of you. Rather, the other person may be able to tell that you are "acting out"—consciously trying to make them feel a certain way about you. And then they will feel, not what you want them to, but rather, that you are an idiot.

This same principle holds true on the level of physical behavior. T'ai-chi-Ch'uan is considered a "phantom style" of kung-fu. This means, among other things, that you try to move and act as little as possible (in the fighting), giving your opponent very little to work with as he is trying to punch you. You will duck only exactly enough to evade the punch and no more. Your own strikes will use only as much movement and tension as is absolutely needed and no more.

In this way, you won't wear yourself out or get lost in the excesses of your own movements. It requires a certain quietness on your part. This is the frustrating part. In the fighting, for example, you get very excited and want to do all sorts of things (like tensing your muscles), and yet you are taught to stay relaxed and fluid. Fighting isn't the same as posing for a Mr. Universe contest. The battle in your learning is really between acting out and being efficient. I think you will find that this is the same battle involved in any learning situation.

Imagine the degree of attention required to ferret out every little bit of acting out, on an intellectual, emotional and physical level. It is a real spring-cleaning. Once all the cleaning is done, then attention can fill every crevice of the body. These little acts, or pre-programmed behaviors, block attention from filling the body and those parts of the body become deadened to your awareness.

If one hand is neglected, or the knees, or the feet, or the shoulder, then the whole body will be inefficient. Your attention must decentralize, leaving its comfortable, secure home in the mind (center of acting) and journey into unknown territories. Those unknown territories are none other than your own self. The intermediate student learns to "see himself."

The Universal Internal Language

All physical sensations, such as balance and pressure, are translated into a common imagery to unify the energy of spontaneous creativity with the senses. (What?) Let's examine this last statement in greater detail as it is an essential lesson for an intermediate student.

The nervous system seems to be divided into three parts. One part receives information (the senses). Another part sends messages to the muscles, glands, etc., to regulate their functions. The third part acts as an intermediary between the two, processing incoming information to properly adjust its outgoing messages. If your eyes see a truck coming at you, the processing centers may determine that the muscles in the leg should cause you to jump away.

That processing must have criteria by which to judge its subsequent outgoing messages. Normally, much of these criteria are biologically inherent in any organism. But we humans go through such socialization that much of the criteria are those of society, superimposed on the innate, biological criteria.

The need to "win" in our society is often not biologically based. That is, it is not based on physical survival per se but on all sorts of status considerations that are very far removed from their simple biological/ethological origins. (Ethology, the study of the evolution of animal behavior, was one of my major studies in college.) Often, the status behaviors don't result in your own well-being. The status criteria are created to fill someone else's need (an advertiser, country, religion, etc.).

In Push Hands we are forced to get back to natural criteria because we are dealing with basic mechanics (including fluid mechanics, as the body is mostly water).

So all the psychological and social investment in building your status to gain the respect of others is irrelevant. If your body is not properly aligned, if you don't compress the partner's force into your root, you won't succeed in pushing him. This is very frustrating.

Experience and Creativity

We need to go back to the original mechanism of perception, processing, then action. In this mechanism, each individual perception is not so distinct from the next. Sounds, sights, smells, balance, pressure, etc., all feel like qualities of the same feeling. The senses seem to have a common identity. In fact, the experiences of the body, such as thoughts, emotions, the will, and so forth, all seem to have the same identity.

And within that identity lies all the information needed for self-knowledge. Push Hands forces us to translate all our sensations into this common identity so they can be simply processed.

To be mechanistic about it, I guess you could say that the common identity is "nerve impulses." But we're not dissecting this from a mechanistic point of view, we're examining it from an experiential point of view. So the above statement about nerve impulses has little meaning, and little use as a teaching device.

I would rather say that the common identity is imagination—creativity. And thus it is empowered by an image, just as our behavior stems from our self-image.

You can develop an imagery and place it in the processing center, thus determining the relationship between the incoming signals and the outgoing actions. So creativity and the senses have an intimate relationship. But usually it's someone else's creativity that has been implanted in you.

Push Hands requires that you experiment with various imageries to see their effects, and enables you to learn about this relationship between "imagination" and "reality." An effect on one has a corresponding effect on the other. They are in balance. This means that you understand how creativity and the senses interact to form your world. You understand that each person has a different mix or balance of these two parts of life and that your sanity and power in life comes from being aware of your own balance.

The student who thinks Push Hands is just a question of pushing techniques will therefore be very frustrated until he looks inward.

Once the senses (internal and external), the will, mind, emotions and creativity are thus unified, geared to each other, it is very difficult to tell where one leaves off and the next begins. This is what is meant by "unifying."

The student actually first learns to isolate each aspect of his being, then develop each aspect and then reunify them all. This is just as you would repair a car by taking apart the engine, for example, cleaning or perhaps replacing the parts and then putting them back together.

Use of Imagery

Push Hands requires an understanding of this process. The experience of the flows of energy, the pressure on the arms, the shifting and turning of the body, the balance of you and your partner, etc., are translated into an imagery. A simple imagery is to imagine any yang aspect of Push Hands (pressure, force coming up from the ground, moving forward) as white, and any yin aspect (lightness, force being grounded and neutralized, moving backward) as black (or you could reverse the black and white).

The Push Hands would be played by concentrating on this moving pattern of black and white. You would soon understand which patterns lead to effective Push Hands. You would also understand which patterns lead to inefficiency and what that means as to what you did wrong.

Soon, the black-and-white pattern will extend into the other person's body (in your "imagination") so that you will feel the intricacy of his pattern of yin and yang, even to the extent of feeling his pattern of attention.

The "criteria" of that imagery (the relationship of the perception and consequent action) must be understood in the same pictorial terms (black-and-white blobs or whatever you choose as the imagery). You can use the imagery of the balloon filled with air (attention). When you are perfectly lined up for a push, it seems as though the balloon is pierced by a needle and the force rushes out. With the "blob" imagery, you can picture this, actually imagining the white force in the balloon flowing out into the partner.

In terms of the frustration about winning or losing, you can see that the real game is in playing with the imagery, not in who gets pushed. It brings you to the state of being a child engaged in play. The children's play allows them to practice "adult" skills.

Push Hands imagery allows us to practice skills few people ever develop. They are the skills of the next stage of our development as humans. If only this were taught in our schools, how different people would be!

Unfortunately, few people are involved in T'ai-chi in the West. And to many of those who are, Push Hands is just "wrestle-mania" and the Form is just learning a mechanical set of movements.

Should You Tell Anyone?

So the "legitimate" student has learned something which is hard to even discuss with his friends. Should he attempt to explain T'ai-chi or keep this aspect of his life hidden? This is an ongoing issue for all the students.

Another problem arises when your friends know that T'ai-chi is a martial art. Men's macho sensitivities may surface when they find out that you are studying kung-fu. Many men react strangely when the subject of martial arts is brought up. They face the same insecurities that you do on first entering fighting class. I'm not as familiar with the reaction of friends of female students, as the women in my school generally do not tell their friends they are studying kung-fu.

Men's reactions are very interesting. They may emit strange grunts and noises and move in unusual ways, perhaps stamping their feet on the ground. It's amazing that a single word, "kung-fu," can have the power to change a person's behavior.

Most students opt to keep their studies a secret. Of course, they have to tell wives or husbands, boyfriends or girlfriends. Male students face a special problem when their wives become jealous of T'ai-chi as if it were another woman. Sometimes a wife refuses to have sex with her husband unless he quits T'ai-chi.

Fear of Mellow

I believe the animosity is not just due to the time the husband spends at class and practicing at home. T'ai-chi makes a person mellow and more relaxed. I believe that many female partners do not want their husbands or boyfriends to be so mellow.

In comparing notes with my male friends over the years, I have concluded that some women seem to prefer a very yang male. This male must offer the element of danger, in the sense that the woman is not sure how stable her mate is. If he were very mellow, kind and loving, there would be no thrill. He must have anger, hostility and to some extent, not be in control of himself. Such women can then have negative feelings about the man and have rich sources of reasons for complaining.

When T'ai-chi dissolves the anger and hostility, then this woman is faced with having to relate to the man as a person, and that is frightening, because it is real. She may have to actually open up her feelings and allow her mate to come close to her soul.

I'm not sure about the dynamics the other way around. The big fear is really facing the other person straight on, and we do all sorts of maneuvering to avoid it.

Several women even told me that they would never become involved with anyone they loved because they wouldn't want to get hurt. I think they are already hurting.

I would certainly appreciate letters from readers concerning this issue. My purpose is not to complain but to make T'ai-chi useful and understandable in our immediate everyday lives. In this way, we can really grow.

Some T'ai-chi students are first exposed to the idea of growing and allowing themselves to change, after they are involved in a relationship with a person who is not willing to grow. The growth of the student is seen as a threat to the stability of the relationship. When the student tells his or her mate about moving blobs of black and white, then the mate feels the student is going off the deep end. The student moves outside of the mate's awareness, outside of the mate's echo of expectations. Since the mate doesn't know about any "outside," he or she feels the student is drifting away to the nether regions.

Building a T'ai-chi Community

A student therefore needs a tremendous amount of self-motivation because he will rarely be cheered on by friends or a mate. And since the schools are very low-key, there isn't the stimulation that comes from shouting and stamping one's feet.

Nowadays the T'ai-chi community is growing, providing its own support network. A marriage has already resulted from two students who met at my school and they just recently had a baby.

Too often, though, students have to divide their lives in two, and keep T'ai-chi out of their social lives as a subject for discussion. Rather, they learn to use T'ai-chi principles in their relationships. They hope that by changing their own patterns of behavior, this will affect people around them.

Expanding Attention

The intermediate student learns to expand his attention. In Push Hands, every part of his body must be alive and active at all times. Typically, when the attention goes to one side, say, to the neutralizing side, the other side "dies." One arm may act to neutralize, but the other just dangles, having been drained of attention.

The student learns that one side acts only in relation to the other side. In this way, the partner's force can be re-channeled back into the partner.

The student's attention must fill the entirety of his world of experience. An event in one place is significant only in regard to events or circumstances in the rest of his field of experience.

The intermediate student should be aware of each body part, his and his partner's balance, his partner's body parts, the eddies and currents of momentum, his and his partner's patterns of attention, the angle of hips, the springy quality of his body, the resiliency of the floor, the pattern of firmness and looseness in his and his partner's arms and many more factors while practicing Push Hands. A change in any one factor affects all the others.

Attention can be easily worn out. When a muscle is worn out we experience soreness. When attention is worn out, we experience frustration. We don't mind the soreness because we know that our muscles will grow as a result of being used. We should not mind the frustration either because it indicates that attention is growing.

The teacher must allow the student to push him from time to time even though the teacher could easily neutralize the student's push. This minimizes frustration and also gives the student good practice.

Teacher-Student Relationships

I mention this because there are some "teachers" who don't teach. They push their students around in Push Hands or beat them soundly in fighting to show how good they are. This serves to impress the student, but what has that student actually learned?

Students have to learn what it feels like to successfully push, kick or punch. When I was a student-teacher at William Chen's school, he didn't want me to duck too often because the students wouldn't get practice in punching. He also didn't want me to hit the student hard or the student would become discouraged. I was supposed to let myself be hit a lot and just learn to internally neutralize the punches. It took a lot of headaches to learn how to do that.

Beginning teachers may become emotionally defensive when one of their students hits them. Instead, they should be proud that they taught that student well.

It's a mistake to try to "prove yourself" to your students. You will be creating an emotionally awkward atmosphere in class. Siimply do the best you can and teach the best you can. Remember that some students may advance beyond you and need a new teacher. What's wrong with that? Being honest about your abilities leads to a comfortable and enjoyable experience as a T'ai-chi teacher.

I heard of one teacher who never actually taught his students how to do Push Hands or fighting. Yet he would do it with them. Naturally, he was much better than they were because they didn't know what they were doing, and they worshipped him for his great abilities. To me, this is dishonest.

So at the intermediate stage of a student's development, these teacher-student issues will come up. The student may start comparing himself to the teacher and feel that he is superior to his teacher. This is especially so in fighting between a much older teacher and a young student, because the student has more stamina. Also, the teacher may spend many hours earning a living and be tired by the time he gets to class. A young student may have fewer responsibilities and be less tired.

But such students should ask themselves, "Is there anything more I can learn from this teacher? Have I really learned all there is to learn from him?"

And if the student has progressed so far with his teacher, doesn't this say something about his teacher's ability to teach? Surely there must be more to learn from his teacher.

Once in awhile, a teacher may play with the student, really tossing him around, to show who is boss. This isn't necessarily done egotistically, but rather to illustrate the potential of Push Hands or fighting and to remind the student that there is always more to learn.

Reinforcing Exercises

I find that at this stage of development, boredom can set in. The student has been practicing for a long time, and progress is relatively slower than at the beginning.

At this stage, I begin to introduce auxiliary exercises, often from other training systems, to augment the teaching:

1. CHANTING

Using drumming and chanting, I teach the students to allow their attention to vibrate along with the combined vibration of the drums, rattles and voices. The attentions of the several students merge, and at that point, all the individual sounds are synchronized into a tight harmony. They learn how attention is a unifying force. The harmony thus produced mimics the harmony of cells and organs in the body.

This harmony on the interpersonal level affects the cells and brings about greater health and relaxation.

This is not a pretty, melodic type of chanting, but a release of whatever sounds happen to come out. At first, the participants try to "sound good" but this creates a mentally driven type of chanting. After awhile, the participants feel free to let out whatever is inside them. The harmony that results is "real" and causes deep effects.

For some people, this type of chanting is the first time they have been able to let go of their attention and allow their attention to move beyond the boundaries of their self-image.

2. APPLE THROWING

During the autumn, many apples fall from the apple trees at the school. The students squat under the trees at night waiting for a crazed T'ai-chi teacher to throw apples at them.

I don't actually hit them with the apples but throw nearby. If a student hears or sees one passing near, he or she jumps up, turns around to face the direction of the throw and remains in that position until another apple lands near him.

This teaches concentration and patience, and strengthens the legs and the senses.

3. THE FOREST WINE CEREMONY

This is a ceremony I pieced together from stories from Taoist ceremonies in ancient China. It is a joyful ritual and one of the most powerfully transforming ceremonies I use in my classes. Juice can be substituted for the wine. Several of my students have stopped drinking alcohol and certainly the use of alcohol is not looked on as favorably now as in the past. If you prefer not to drink wine, the juice serves just as well.

The Forest Wine Ceremony is one of those charming little traditions seeping out of an obscure past just when needed:

Imagine night in a deep forest in ancient China, and a small campfire near a cold mountain stream. Several followers of Taoism sit around the fire, laughing over the various ways they fooled their teachers in order to escape garbage duty. They are poor, their practice difficult, and the everyday problems of life are always present.

A fair volume of extremely cheap, slightly sweet wine is brought out, along with a large, heavy ceramic chalice, and the Taoist students hurriedly try to think of things to be thankful for. For each expression of gratitude the student is allowed to take a sip of the sacred fluid.

For example, the first fellow holds up the chalice and speaks: "I am thankful our teacher is too old to hit us hard." He takes a sip, places the chalice on the ground, places the palms of his hands down on either side of it, and the entire company bows.

The chalice is then placed before the next participant. She raises it and says: "I am thankful for spending time in this beautiful forest with such good friends." She takes a sip, places the chalice on the ground, places her hands on either side, and again, all bow. And so it goes, around and around. (In an alternative method, each student holds his own cup and they all sip together.)

There are several rules and methods to this seemingly simple ceremony. The most obvious, of course, is trying to think of as many things to be thankful for as possible, so the wine can continue going around the circle.

The most obvious difficulty is being able to talk coherently after the first few pourings of the goblet.

You may be thankful for the animals of the forest, your health, your teachers, the wine, vitamins, gravity or breath fresheners. Whether your gratitude is serious or humorous, it gets you a sip. In fact, if you can make the others laugh, you might be able to sneak an extra gulp without being noticed.

Little side comments are allowed and, in fact, are an important part of the ceremony. A master of this ceremony would be noted for his or her incisive side comments.

When the goblet is placed on the ground, prior to bowing, the hands of the speaker are placed on the ground for two important reasons. The first is that each thank you is really a thanks to the earth, the Mother of All. The second reason is that coordination may become difficult after the first few rounds. Without well-grounded hands, the forward momentum of the bow may provide the speaker's face with a dunking.

After all have given their thanks for the good things in life, there may still be some wine left. It would not be inappropriate at that point to give thanks for the mishaps of life as well. They, too, are part of the human experience and deserve at least a sip of recognition.

Each participant sips by himself while the others watch. After all, we must ultimately depend on ourselves, and our connection to the earth, to deal with life's experiences. Yet our friends can be there to support, comfort and teach us and thus the entire circle bows in support of the speaker.

When each person has his own cup, all sip together. This allows the drinking to take place at a faster pace. I'm sure there is some rationale to explain why this method also is sacred. (Let me know if you think of something.)

After each sip, the chalice is placed on the earth. We must not instantly be grabbing for the rewards, the goals, the next step. Time is needed for meditation, for release and relaxation. Even the brain needs periodic resting; constant thinking, like constant drinking, drains and damages the rest of our being.

The campfire does more than warm the surrounding bodies. Fire represents the light, the insight gained by reflection on our lives. It is easy to be caught up in complaining. There is so much more we would like to have, or to be. And yet, there is so much we have to be thankful for.

We are alive; we live on a beautiful planet, during a crucial, exciting period in history. Knowledge, both "inner" and "outer," surrounds us, to be plucked from the library, university, T'ai-chi school and, of course, from our own hearts. We have less to fear from disease, invasion and starvation than at most times in history. And so, what are you doing with your life? The fire represents the vision of your life and your place in the destiny of this living planet.

This ceremony tends to bring out the spirit of each person clearly. By words, intonations, the seriousness, the laughter, even the burping, the barriers between the circle's members melt away. The warmth of the fire blends with the warmth of emotion.

Obviously, the fire should be in a pit, dug into the earth itself. But a candle may have to be used as a substitute if the ceremony is done indoors. In a forest, the campfire provides an oasis of light in the vast blackness of the wooded night. It seems like a small, lighted circle of laughing forest spirits embodied in human flesh. How warm a feeling it is to realize that you are part of this!

For how many millions of years have beings sat around campfires, laughing and enjoying each other's company? Suddenly there is the realization that you are connected to all such ancestry in spirit. Each has thanked the earth in his own way. And then the realization hits that this all may end in our own generation. After the thanks, how can we express our responsibility to our Mother Earth, to the source of life?

With our friends, our circle, our tiny light within the forest, we proclaim our gratitude to all creatures, great and small, who might be listening.

4. DREAMWORK

I use dreaming as a way of breaking the barrier between the waking and sleeping states. This provides the student with full access to his subconscious.

The waking state is characterized by the strict organization of raw perception into logical forms. In the sleeping or dreaming state, perception is organized biologically. The relevance of incoming information is with respect to the biological functioning of the body.

Of course, logic still has some degree of hold on us even in dreaming, and biology still holds some sway in waking. But our culture has separated these ways of organizing incoming data about as far as they can be separated.

The "point of intersection" of the two states is a place of great power. It is the "place" where transformation happens.

We begin this work by going over the Form in our minds once a day while sitting. As we imagine ourselves doing the Form, we breathe according to the proper sequence of breaths. Students find it almost as hard to do this as it was first learning the Form.

You must be aware of the movement of all parts of the body, the momentum, weight distribution, etc., as if you were physically doing the Form.

The student also does this in bed, just before going to sleep, with the intention of practicing the Form in dreams.

On waking up the next morning, the student stands up (while still half asleep), moves to a convenient place and practices the Form, trying to maintain his half-asleep state.

Then he relaxes and tries to remember if he did, indeed, do the Form in his dreams. He may find that, while he did remember to practice the Form in the dreams, there were other people in the dream and he felt uncomfortable practicing with them around and soon forgot about the Form. Or, while he began the Form, he was distracted by something and his dream changed.

Obviously, to practice the Form in dreams, you must be aware that you are dreaming and you must remember what you are supposed to do. This requires bringing the waking state into the sleeping state.

On the other hand, the student brings the sleeping state into the waking state as follows: While physically practicing the Form, he allows himself to drift into a dreaming awareness. Dream images flow past his mind even while his eyes are open. He realizes that the actions in the dream images are geared to his physical movements in the Form, in the same way that the movements of one part of the body are geared to the movements of all the other parts.

Double Awareness

Once a student gains proficiency at practicing the Form while dreaming, he then splits his awareness in two. While dreaming, he is aware of the dream on the one hand, and of his body, lying on the bed, on the other hand.

Practicing this double awareness can be enhanced as follows: He holds something (I used a small hairbrush) in his hand all during the night. The hairbrush I used sticks the hand with its bristles so you can feel it easily as you sleep. It is not easy to hold something when you sleep so you may use a rubber band around your hand to hold it in place.

In this way, your attention will easily go to the brush while dreaming and you can hover between awareness of the dream scene and the brush. You keep practicing this until your awareness of both is solid. That is, you really feel you are in the dream scene with the full solidity of your body. You also feel the realness, the solidity of the brush in your hand and your body lying in bed.

This double awareness may be your first glimpse into holographic attention in which the attention is decentralized but balanced and controlled by body-mind. It allows you to start to perceive the whole of you, including that vast area beyond logical structures.

Dream Guide

Another technique some people use is to find a guide in the dreams. You place a figurine of some kind beside the bed. This will be the waking form of your guide. Care should be taken to find one that feels right. I used "Pepito," a big stuffed mouse with big ears, holding a bow and an arrow piercing a red felt heart. It also had a little top hat.

You try to find your guide in the dreams, but remember that it may appear in a different form. When you find it, you can ask it questions and try to remember the answers when you wake up. Anything that happens after you ask the question is the answer. The trick is to know what questions to ask, and that you will just have to experiment with.

More Advanced Dreamwork

The next step is to develop higher resolution of attention while dreaming. You can place the brush on various parts of the body, for example. Then (and this is very important), "trace" the connection between the feeling of the brush and the dream images. There will be a definite connection. When you concentrate on both at the same time, and hold both experiences steady, a connection will become apparent in your feelings.

Then trace the feeling of your hand lying on the bed, a hair on your nose, etc., to the dream images. This process may take years but it will open up the inner connections to your conscious awareness.

Then, during the day, notice those same inner connections and how they are affected by your everyday activities.

At this point you may find it hard to distinguish whether you are awake or asleep. But waking and sleeping will no longer be such a crucial criterion. You will realize that the more important consideration is to be *aware*.

Dreaming will become a power which is always accessible to you and waking will be your connection to this particular world. Dreaming will be the motor that energizes you, and waking the chassis of the machine that channels that power. It will no longer be a question of whether your eyes are open or closed. You will develop new eyes that will always be open.

The next step is to practice other forms in the dreams—the animal forms (snake, tiger, mantis, monkey, crane and drunken). Obviously, you can become an animal in the dreams and shed the limitations of the human body.

You can also practice Push Hands and fighting with "dream partners," or go to classes with a "dream teacher." Remember that on this level, awareness is not limited to the boundaries of your physical body.

Dreamwork reveals how the separation of your conscious and subconscious robs you of power. It reunites forgotten parts of yourself so that you can face the world as a whole person.

Warning

As in all such work, there is a warning: It must all be done with an attitude of emptiness. And it must be conducted with the feeling that this is a normal, everyday, ordinary thing and not some adventure into the wild blue yonder.

Dreamwork can make you sensitive and unsure. Much of it requires either a good teacher to whom you can turn, or a very stable practitioner.

It is important to maintain the activities you are used to and maintain the human relationships that bring you stability. Dreamwork should not be practiced when going through difficult emotional times.

The more powerful a practice is, the more stability you need around you. It is too easy to develop an attitude of aloofness. ("I'm doing such advanced practices and my friends are so unadvanced.") This is simply arrogance. If you become arrogant as a result of any practice, then obviously that practice has done you more harm than good.

Dreaming the Body

When connections between dream images and body feelings have been made, then you can drop the images and dream the body. In this case, your dreaming consists of awareness of the body's biological functioning. You don't need to represent this functioning in terms of dream images. You are aware of the source of much of the images.

At this stage, you can tune your focus of attention down to smaller and smaller parts of the body, even to the individual cells. It is your own microscope, made out of attention.

It will take a long time to understand the relationship of what you experience "down there" to activities in your everyday life. Each motion, thought, emotion, perception affects each part of the body. When you become aware of how an experience or activity affects the inner, cellular world, you will know how to conduct your life for maximum health and well-being.

Actually, your very behavior will stem from such awareness and from the attempt to maintain an inner balance and harmony. The inner balance thus created (or allowed to happen naturally) will be reflected in the balance and harmony of your everyday life. So the "inner" world and "outer" world will no longer seem so distinct. Your self-image as flesh and thoughts bound by your skin will no longer seem valid. This awareness of oneself will stem from that balance and harmony of the inner and outer worlds. You will become the gatekeeper.

Not Being There

The intermediate student must also learn to "not be there." This means that he must learn to be, not the winner of a contest, but an efficient organism. His "fashioned creature" is dropped as he develops the "attitude of emptiness."

I remember one particular student who went through such a transition. In the beginning, he reacted to my correcting his posture and hand positions by rapidly changing his position the way he thought I wanted him to change. In other words, as soon as I touched him to make the correction, he jerked his arm as if to "help me" put him in the right position.

This made it more difficult as, of course, he didn't really know how I was going to correct him. Yet this behavior was so much part of his personality that I didn't want to challenge him on it too soon, because it would cut too close to his self-image.

Finally, I told him to stop. When he did the Form, I kept correcting a particular tension in his back which was also deep-seated.

After completing the Form, he told me that not tensing in the way he was used to made him feel "not there." The tension made him feel "there." He said being "not there" was a fearful experience to him. I assured him that such an experience is, indeed, what we want in T'ai-chi.

Obviously the tension was an ineffective behavior because it had no practical purpose. But these behaviors (the tension and jerking his arm when I tried to correct him) served the purpose of reenforcing the feeling of the fashioned creature. That creature is fashioned out of precisely such behaviors.

The Fashioned Creature Is Not There

If the student identifies with the fashioned creature, then when he begins to drop the inefficient behaviors, he will truly feel "not there." Yet, he experiences the same world around him as before.

The problem is that if his motivation for practicing T'ai-chi has been to help reenforce the fashioned creature, he may then become lazy. When the "talons" of his attention are released from the fashioned creature, they may try to grab onto something else. The teacher must direct those talons to make sure they don't grab onto yet another fashioned creature.

The student's attention must then be connected to the world around and inside him, not the social world, but the natural world.

The truth of the matter is that he really "isn't here." There is a Zen saying,

"There is suffering but nobody who suffers it," and I might add, "There is joy but nobody who enjoys it." The joy and the suffering themselves are all the "you" there is. You are all of your experiences and the balance among those experiences.

The intermediate student must learn that balance by letting go of rigid identity. The Push Hands helps by blending the attentions of two people together until individual boundaries are meaningless.

The fighting helps even more. Many of the behaviors composing the fashioned creature are ways of being false. In other words, we want to do something and are told we cannot. So we find ways around it by "taking out our frustrations" in dishonest, re-directed behavior.

In the fighting this is not possible. Someone is bashing you in the head. You simply have to duck and punch or kick back. It is very direct with no room for false behaviors. You must function efficiently, appropriately for the situation, and concentrate on the here and now. The fashioned creature simply cannot do this because its very existence is based on the lack of directness. You must really be "not there" in fighting. In a sense being "not there" really means "being here."

Once the fashioned creature is dropped, the student will display fewer stereotyped behaviors and repeat fewer stereotyped expressions. (Do you know people who repeat the same expressions over and over again?) In fact, the fashioned creature may be thought of as the cork in the hole through which the earth's creativity tries to flow.

At times, that cork pops, resulting in disorientation or even a "nervous breakdown." In this case, the person is not practiced at channeling creativity and is utterly terrified that the fashioned creature is lost. Power is pouring through but that person has no way of using it.

Balancing Yin and Yang

Another transition in this intermediate stage is the balancing of yin and yang. For some students this will require more yang and for others, more yin. I was very yin before learning T'ai-chi-Ch'uan, very passive. The fighting was difficult for me because I didn't enjoy hitting anyone. (Few people do.)

Even though I knew they wouldn't be hurt (because of their protective padding), I was very unenthusiastic about hitting. But I was also unaggressive in other ways (socially for example) and this caused problems in my life. While I thought of myself as being a pacifist and therefore more "pure," I was actually just unbalanced.

I soon understood this but could not find any practice powerful enough for rebalancing until I discovered the fighting.

For people who are *too* aggressive, the Form may be the more powerful tool for rebalancing. Yet the fighting also can serve to rebalance someone who is too aggressive. If you are tense and angry in fighting, you bind yourself up and are too slow. Also, your attention is bound up and you can't notice the subtleties of what your partner is doing. Consequently, you get hit more.

At each stage of T'ai-chi-Ch'uan practice, a balance of yin and yang is needed and in fighting, the consequences of imbalance are greater—the stakes are higher.

The yin student learns the power of yang and the yang student learns the power of yin. When you reach the center of that balance, you are "not there," which is the same as saying that you are honest.

The next stage of a student's development is filled with exploration, risks and the realization that no matter how much you learn about T'ai-chi-Ch'uan, it is insignificant compared to what there is to learn. The advanced student can see the absurdity of his impatience and begins to appreciate the simple, everyday things of life.

CHAPTER 20
THE ADVANCED STUDENT

What determines a beginning or advanced student is not the level of the subject he is studying but the depth of his attainment in that subject. Each student is at a particular level with each of the subjects he is learning. There are beginning students of fighting or Chi-gung as well as of the Form. As the student begins the next level of T'ai-chi-Ch'uan in subject matter, he feels as awkward and unprepared as the first day he walked into the school.

At the beginning level, the student learns the body mechanics of the Form, the breathing sequence, compression and expansion of the body, correct posture and how to connect attention to the flow of momentum.

The intermediate stage includes practicing the Form in dreamwork, working out the pathways of momentum and attention, lining up attention with gravity, eliminating any minute tensions that interfere with the fluidity of the body, and developing holographic attention which is decentralized throughout the body. He must also begin to bring these principles of movement into his everyday life so that his life becomes a T'ai-chi Form.

Now, what is left for the advanced student? At this point, the student must be able to focus attention down to the cellular level, to be aware of the "momentum" of cellular activity. This momentum is heavily influenced by such things as breathing dynamics, food intake, emotions, and so forth. While practicing the Form, this student becomes aware of the Form's effect on the cellular momentum.

When the student's Form is corrected or when he experiments with doing the Form in a new way, he is interested in how that affects cellular momentum.

In this way, he can see how the Form revitalizes his body from the cellular level on up. The cells actually teach him the correct way of doing the Form as he can sense their "approval" of the correctly practiced Form. This approval is evident in the cells' ease in functioning.

At the muscular level, the ease of movement allows the muscles to teach the student. He becomes aware of the pattern of energy in other creatures, which allows him to learn from them just as he learns from his own body.

While the beginning and intermediate student learns from the teacher, the advanced student learns from everything. Rather than learning how to "do" the Form, Push Hands and other practices, he learns from "doing."

When the advanced student reads an article about T'ai-chi, he doesn't store the fact in his memory to increase his knowledge. Rather, he compares what the author wrote to his own inner experiences. In this way he can tell if the author is merely spouting dogma or describing his inner awareness.

It is as if you were blind and needed someone else to describe the scenery to you. But then you regain your sight and don't need anyone to describe the scenery anymore. You may have learned many descriptive terms of the scenery when you were blind, but now you don't need them.

Yet, there may be those who think that the descriptive terms are the issue. They are not interested in the scenery itself but have built a comfortable world of descriptive phrases, and love to talk. Returning to the scenery can be a lonely trek if your fellows are all back home talking away. But the advanced student must make this trek.

I wrote a song about this process for my book *May I Have Your Attention?* (self-published, 1981):

THE GATEKEEPER

There is a story that is told
To every baby born
They all must memorize it
Though the tale is old and worn
It tells them who they are and who they can be
Though it's really just a story
We convince them that it's real

(chorus):
Are you inside looking out?
Are you outside looking in?
The gatekeeper blocks not the way
The whole world is his kin
Are you troubled by the world?
Are you troubled by yourself?
The true gatekeeper has no gate
No worries and no wealth

A little boy is reaching out
Can you resist his pleas?

He lost his friends so long ago
He lost his family
The world is unfamiliar
Its lights shine cold and bleak
There is no food for him to eat
His spirit's growing weak

A boy and girl were split apart
When he went off to fight
His days were spent in battle
Unhappy was the night
They never got together
Though I swear that it is true
They wear the same pajamas
This young lover and you

(repeat chorus)

An island rests upon the sea
Its shores are filled with rocks
The breakers smash upon them
And break apart the docks
No ship will venture near it
They shun its stormy seas
One day the weather will abide
And ships will dock with ease

Your name is written on a stone
Its sound will make you wise
But the tablet rests inside a cave
Filled with howling cries
You may traverse the darkness
Without a bit of fear
The cries will lead you to your name
And the walls will disappear

(repeat chorus)

The forest is a magic land
With many things to see
The bushes and the animals
And climbing in the trees
But some remain atop the trees
And never do come down
We will leave them for the vultures
And dance upon the ground

A little rabbit sticks its head
Out of the bushy fern
So many years have passed
And still it waits for your return
The forest it is dying
It withers by the day
But it will be the rabbit
Who rests upon your grave

Your Spirit Emerges

The rabbit in this song is your own spirit. At the advanced stage, the T'ai-chi practices become the forest within which you can find the rabbit. This discipline is no longer played to enhance the self-image but to fold back this image to find one's spirit.

Fighting, for example, is no longer practiced to "get that person before he gets me," but to develop your skill, attention and relaxation so your spirit can come through and take over.

In this case, the spirit merely means your true nature when fear, anger, tension and pain are dissolved.

This is a dangerous time for the student. For much of his life, his enthusiasm for living may have come from a desire to enhance his self-image in the eyes of others and, in this way, to feel better about himself.

When his enthusiasm is no longer tied to his self-image, he may become listless and indecisive. This period may last several months, resulting, perhaps, in a much-needed rest. But then that original spirit comes shining through, the joy of living for itself, and the real T'ai-chi-Ch'uan practice can begin.

During the transitional period, the student may feel that he "just doesn't care about anything." At this time the fighting is a very useful practice because it gives him something to care about (not having his head punched in).

The student is in a very valuable position at this point in fighting. He has given up striving to enhance his self-image, yet he must strive to protect his physical well-being. This sets the tone for the rest of his practice—learning T'ai-chi for physical, emotional and spiritual well-being rather than to enhance the self-image.

So when a student starts to become listless, the teacher should do the following:

1. Let him be listless for a month or so to make sure his self-image is losing its power.
2. Get the student involved in fighting, to focus his attention on his survival.

You may find that a lot of the nonsense associated with the self-image will simply drop away at this point. The student's ability to grow and learn is then magnified. Rather than reinforcing what he is, the student can now work towards what he can become.

Accepting Your Body-Mind

Another problem that may arise at this point is that the body-mind has gained in power relative to the thinking-mind. Body-mind is now learning and growing quickly.

Yet the student may still associate learning with thinking (learning facts). The body-mind may be perceived as a "foreign" body, as something not of himself. He may not be aware that he is learning anything, because he does not recognize the part of himself that is doing the learning.

A student may be progressing rapidly and yet feel that he is not getting anywhere. This reminds me of a woman who is very attractive but doesn't think she is. Some men feel awkward around her because of her beauty. The woman interprets the awkwardness as the man not liking her, which further reinforces her feeling that she is not desired.

Or, the man may have a pained expression while looking at her because he feels, "She could never like me." The woman may interpret the facial expression as, "I don't like that woman." This dynamic works the opposite way as well.

The T'ai-chi student may have similar difficulty in dealing with the body-mind, which is so much more beautiful (skilled) than his self-image—especially if he tends to put himself down a lot. It may be hard for him to accept this beautiful body-mind as part of himself. This student has to learn to "be himself," to accept the parts of himself.

That integration is what gives him power. That is when his spirit comes shining through. It is like the power that results in finally finding out that the woman (or man) you like likes you too. There's a lot of smiling as a result and laughing, too. You laugh at the foolishness of your negative self-image.

Yet some people perform one last maneuver to prevent the integration of body-mind. They still consider body-mind to be separate but feel it is God, or the voice of someone from the spirit world speaking through them. They call it anything but a natural part of themselves.

Luckily, the T'ai-chi discipline tends to prevent such maneuvering and keeps the student down-to-earth. And should the student become egotistical about having such a wonderful part of himself, the fighting class will keep him humble.

The Feeling Content of Perception

Along with the integration of thinking-mind and body-mind comes the integration of conscious-subconscious states, and sleeping and waking states.

It also puts an end to the separation of "inner" and "outer." When we see objects in the world we are, of course, experiencing our own internal nervous system at work. Yet we project this vision onto a theoretical "outside" world, and that seems to work for us in a practical sense.

Yet by doing so, we may also deny the actual experience of what we see. Each perception triggers a whole series of changes within our bodies. Children are aware of this "feeling" content of perception. But as we get older, we tend to separate the feelings that result from a perception from the perception itself.

This is done because we live in a society that ignores the relationship between our internal and external environments. Our institutions and customs do not take this relationship into account. Our religious systems worship the ability to maintain such a separation, and consider that separation the mark of an intelligent, civilized society.

Yet our physical and emotional (and even mental) states suffer, because such a separation denies reality.

The advanced T'ai-chi student is aware of the relationship of the internal and external states. He is aware that this relationship is the source of biological behavior on cellular, individual and ecological levels. The formalized logic and language we humans have developed could be used to enhance the biological mechanism, but instead they have "replaced" it.

Now the advanced student must seek a new compromise between this biological necessity and the requirements of society. This may require a shift in relationships, activities and life-style. Any recovering alcoholic understands this. Such a person is in a difficult position because he can now vividly feel the effects of his self-destructive behavior. The excuse that he "must" do it because that's what everyone does, doesn't help. He can no longer numb himself to what he is doing to himself.

Re-integrating Your Parts

The advanced student can also feel the joy of his body functioning in a healthy way, the "partying of his cells." This makes his decision to devote himself to T'ai-chi much easier.

It is to the credit of those who invented and developed T'ai-chi that it is designed to push the student to making a choice with only one possible outcome.

The student "chooses" to identify, not with his mind or any one part of himself, but with the whole of his experience. He sees how integrated all the parts of his experience are. Any divisions are obviously artificial, especially the division of "self" and "other."

The advanced student becomes an instrument of promoting harmony in the world, a diplomat to end the war of humans against nature. His own internal war has ended. When he speaks, it is body-mind that is speaking. The thinking-mind merely serves as translator. There is no longer a need to rehearse his every thought and move. In other words, he is truly free.

He trusts his competence. He is no longer a mere little pimple on the face of the earth, but a natural extension of the earth, a completely connected part of it. When he acts or speaks, the earth backs him up.

This is as it should be. He is no superman but, rather, an ordinary creature of the earth—a magical animal of the forest.

This Means You!

At this point it would be appropriate to point out how the pronoun "he," used for convenience in writing, may subconsciously make women feel they are excluded. Of course, any reference to "he," equally applies to "she." In my book *May I Have Your Attention?*, I use the pronoun "she" almost exclusively. Readers tell me that they feel jolted by this but they like the effect.

In what ways do we feel that we could not be an advanced student? Do you feel you could not attain that level of advancement?

Remember that when you were a fetus, and then an infant, you were at, or close to, that level. Certainly you could return to what you were originally, but now with the added benefit of your years of experience.

It is our assumptions which keep us from becoming all we were meant to be. We feel, "This level can only be reached by a very few people."

Stepping Behind Your Assumptions

To "return" to your advanced level, you must step behind your assumptions. You must go behind the stage where all the performers are acting their best, to see what really goes on when the curtain is closed.

Assumptions are a façade and behind that façade is your power. The advanced student has seen behind the façade of his own assumptions. There, he has found the beginnings of the trail leading to his own true self and to his destiny in this life. His walk back along that trail is conducted in a specific way. First of all, he must learn to "appreciate himself." This means that he remembers all the ways he has tried to learn, grow and develop skills. He remembers the complex route that brought him from his earliest years to this particular time and stage of development.

He understands the limitations he had to work with, both physical and psychological, and the limitations on his opportunities for learning.

Walking on this path requires remembering the quality of self-image at each stage of his life, and how that self-image affected his learning.

Perhaps an episode in his life that seemed negative at the time will now be remembered as a learning experience necessary to bring him to where he is now.

Then he realizes that there was an unseen craftsman behind all this, one who may have even pushed him into difficult experiences in order to learn.

This craftsman—his original, creative spirit—tried to mold an effective mind and body, an effective life, to provide a safe and durable forum for it to emerge into the world.

Now the advanced student remembers that purpose and how it was accomplished (to whatever degree it was, in fact, accomplished). He remembers who he is and what he has created. He no longer mistakes what he has created, for his true self.

Attitude of Emptiness

At this point the "attitude of emptiness" becomes very important. The opposite attitude, that of filling things up or forcing things to happen, keeps your eyes turned away from the path that leads back to your creative spirit.

Students are always amazed that when they feel as if they haven't done anything, that's when the most power comes out. That's when they are most in balance.

This empty feeling allows the creative spirit to gush through, and that spirit, that energy, is very powerful. Have you ever been overwhelmed with feeling when being with a lover and then felt you had to explain yourself or to say something that would present a rationale as to why you are feeling so good? Why couldn't you allow that overwhelming feeling to overwhelm you, and accept such a wonderful gift without reservation? The attitude of emptiness is the acceptance that allows joy to flow through one's life.

It is as if the student had brought in a huge crew with heavy equipment to cut a water tunnel through underground rock and power an electric plant. But now, all the equipment and personnel must be removed before the water can flow through. Only then will electricity be produced. If the water flows through before the people and equipment are removed, there will be much damage and loss of life and the generators will be clogged with the bodies and equipment.

The student's ability to accept T'ai-chi-Ch'uan as a normal down-to-earth part of his life is the emptiness. When he becomes too cocky, too enamored or concerned with what he is doing, he clogs his tunnels. How can the earth enjoy itself through you when you are so concerned with your every move that you continually find reasons not to be happy?

Myth as a Tool

The entire process of learning described thus far in this chapter, I call "creating a myth, becoming the myth and vanishing without a trace." The student first becomes interested in T'ai-chi because he hopes to enhance his self-image, "creating a myth." Perhaps he has seen kung-fu movies and imagines himself as one of the characters.

He then becomes involved in it, practicing diligently, "becoming the myth." He feels he is now a "T'ai-chi person." He has all sorts of ideas of what that means, and strives to behave and think as a T'ai-chi person would, perhaps saying key phrases and walking in such and such a way.

But then he must vanish without a trace. He must let go of that self-image to become his real self. The student doesn't really know what being a T'ai-chi person means. He only knows his preconceived ideas. But what he is about to experience will probably be outside his present knowledge and awareness. Thus he must let go of his preconceived ideas, to experience something new. The mythological figure he has striven to become must disappear. In this way, he can be empty so his real self can shine through. His T'ai-chi practice has served to integrate mind and body-mind, conscious and subconscious. The myth was his magical flying carpet to bring him a step further in his growth. But the myth must not be taken as the goal.

This three-part-myth process is conducted on a more sophisticated level as well. The advanced student now uses it as the final tool to craft his life.

Once he understands the destiny of his life, his vision, this tool is used to accomplish that destiny.

Let's say his vision is to help protect the environment. He views the world around him as a Push Hands game with an eye to balance and leverage. Where can he, as an individual, have the most leverage in his goal? Is it by joining a group, creating a teaching situation, becoming politically involved? Where is the sensitive point in the world around him that would most respond to his input?

He then must craft his life, behavior and image to effect that leverage point. His very interactions with people are used to carry out his vision.

Vanishing without a trace, in this case, simply means that you remain the craftsman of your life to achieve your vision, and you do not allow the tools of your trade (assumptions, titles, ideas, etc.) to control you. Remembering that you are an animal of the forest wearing clothes is a great help. Allow yourself to be foolish and make mistakes.

The Animal Man

Let me use my work as an example. When I was graduated from college, my vision was to protect the earth from destruction. I created a teaching vehicle, a series of live animal programs called "The Animal Man," which were presented as entertaining auditorium shows. This involved bringing live reptiles and amphibians into the school where I taught and discussing their ecology, evolution, behavior and protection.

But it involved much more. Interweaving the zoological information were stories and ideas that presented a new perspective, an alternative way of looking at things.

As an example, I show the Southern pine snake which has many ways to protect itself. It's camouflaged as the sand and rocks where it lives. It hisses and strikes (but with its mouth closed—a bluff). It wiggles its tail in pebbles and dead leaves to sound like a poisonous rattlesnake although the pine snake is not poisonous. And it can send out a disagreeable smell like a skunk. So it is a bluffing snake.

A big, powerful snake like a python doesn't go through all this bluffing. It doesn't need to. Who would want to bother a twenty-foot python?

So snakes are very similar to people. The ones that are really scared inside make a lot of noise and act like big shots. The ones that are confident of themselves just take it easy.

This is how I explain the protection of a pine snake. Yet it also (hopefully) blows the game of the big shots in the class and gives the children who are intimidated by the bullies, a new perspective.

When I first bring out the gopher snake, it wiggles around a lot and the audience leans far back. But soon, the snake wiggles its tail around my nose and the audience gets a more lighthearted feeling for the snake. When I ask for volunteers to hold it, almost every child raises his or her hand.

Learning to Fear

The fear of snakes is a learned fear. In young audiences, the children seem as though their world has come to an end if they are not chosen to hold the snake. The older the people in the audience, the fewer the hands that are raised. I have witnessed many little incidents among members of the audience that gave me valuable insights into their fears.

In one junior high school I witnessed a particularly good example. One girl nearly leapt out of her seat when it came time to hold the snake, raising her hand to be picked. Then she noticed all the girls around her making sounds that indicated their disgust at the very thought of holding the snake. I watched the girl as she froze, hand still in the air and glanced around her. She heard the boys commenting on how girls are so squeamish. Suddenly her hand came down and she, too, made the squeamish noises of the other girls.

She saw that to "be a girl" among her peers meant to be afraid of snakes. Although she wanted very much to hold the snake, she also wanted to be considered a "girl." She wanted to become the myth of a "girl." In how many ways have we created or accepted myths and become those myths?

At the high school level, only about one quarter of the students raise their hands.

Many fears are learned. Some are not. I doubt that the fear of a pouncing tiger has to be learned, especially if it is pouncing on you! But there are people who are frightened of even looking at a picture of a snake. Or they are frightened of meeting people, of trying new things, and of many other activities which are not life-threatening.

By allowing the children to face their fear of the snake and find out that their fear is actually hiding their joy, the animal programs serve as a vehicle for inner transformation—and the teachers understand this.

A friend of mine, Bill Elwell, does the same thing but with fire-walking. He gives a four-hour workshop on overcoming fear, ending with the participants walking barefoot over hot coals.

Young children have been only partially "educated" into fear. They are still able to take it as a joke. That is, the feeling of fear itself does not have such a strong control over their behavior that it would preclude trying activities we consider dangerous.

We teach children to be afraid. We teach them to lose their feeling of power. Often we teach them to fear things we are prejudiced against rather than things that are truly dangerous. To see a three-year-old in fear of the world around her is a sorrowful sight. Yet the three-year-olds who are adventurous, alert, joyful and loving show that unreasonable fear does not have to be a part of childhood.

Transmitting Your Own Fears to Children

One summer I had a booth at a fair. A Polaroid camera was set up, pointing to a large, wicker fan chair. For a small fee, I would photograph a person sitting in the chair with a boa constrictor around his neck.

Luckily, a beer vendor was close to my booth. I would wait until an unsuspecting person had finished four or five glasses of beer and then ask him if he would like a picture. In his altered state of consciousness, he would usually agree. If not, his friends would goad him into it.

I noticed many mothers walking with their children. The children usually saw the snake first. Their eyes would light up as they ran over to the exhibit to get a closer look. At some point, the mother would also notice the snake, and scream and pull her child away.

The child would then scream, not at the snake, but at being tugged so hard by his mother. The mother would scream again, commenting on how disgusting the snake was and then tell the child not to go near it. At that point, the child would scream again, this time at the snake, and thus learn fear from his mother.

From that point on, the child would remember the fear of his mother whenever he came across a snake. That fear would be stamped on the child.

The real highlight of "The Animal Man" show is when I ask for volunteers from among the teachers. Each class wants its teacher to hold the snake. Some teachers will come up even though they are afraid, just to avoid transmitting their fear to the children. (They also come up because if they showed a fear of snakes, there's no telling what tricks the children in their class might pull.)

Effects of Fear

Fear has severe effects on the body. The child at the fair became tense when he heard his mother scream. Fear causes tension. And tension injures the body. It constricts the blood vessels, preventing oxygen and nutrients from reaching the cells. It drains the body of energy and is a cause of high blood pressure and heart attacks. It causes headaches, affects our moods and prevents us from reaching a calm, peaceful state. Tension even deprives us of rest when we sleep.

The child at the fair remembered not only the facts about the incident but also the feeling of tension. So that pattern of tension would repeat itself every time he saw a snake. He probably would not react as severely as the first time, but on a more subtle level the sight of a snake would trigger his muscles to repeat his pattern of tension.

If we imagine how many thousands of such episodes in one's life there may be, we begin to understand the complexity of fear.

My animal programs suggest to the audiences that they need not fear, or at least they need not allow fear to control their lives. Some of the children who come up to hold the snake are actually afraid of it. I point this out to the audience after the volunteers have returned to their seats. I explain that, even though they were afraid of the snake, they didn't let their fear stop them. Now, at least, they know what a snake feels like. If this were a poisonous snake, it would make sense not to come up. But these are all harmless.

I suggest that the next time I bring out a snake, even those who are afraid of it can come up. Otherwise, if you let your fear stop you, you may never know what a snake is like.

I mention the poisonous snakes to show that sometimes fear is legitimate. There is a difference between legitimate fear and unfounded fear.

Sneaky Teachings

When I take out the boa, I explain that snakes have many more bones than humans. They can move each bone a little and thereby curl up into unusual shapes. They also have loose muscles, whereas people often have tense muscles. We worry about things. But a snake is too stupid to worry, so it's always relaxed.

Then I tell them about T'ai-chi and how it is used to relax. By talking about the boa, I am able then to talk about the students themselves but in a non-threatening, unobtrusive way.

I find the leverage points in their feelings, in their fears and concerns and use them to open the students up to a new perspective.

In this way, I am fulfilling my original vision by teaching about ecology, but more importantly, by suggesting a new way of life, one more in keeping with living in harmony.

Turning Fear into Joy

The power of the program lies in turning fear into joy. At first, many of the children are afraid of the animals (lizards, turtles, tortoises, toads, etc., are also included). I handle the animals and relate to them in such a way that it is obvious they are gentle and friendly. Then the children can see the beauty of the animals. They can see that their own fear hid the beauty.

Typically, a small child will walk up to the front of the room and tremble as he pets a snake. Then suddenly he laughs, jumps up and down, returns to his seat and proceeds to tell his friends how it felt.

It is a status symbol to be picked to pet the snake. I want them to feel that liking animals is "in." When the children walk into the auditorium, I watch their interpersonal dynamics and try to detect their relative social statuses in regards to their popularity in school. I make sure to invite to the stage a representative sprinkling of all status levels. I bring up those who seem unpopular to give them more popularity, those who seem popular to show that this is a "popular" thing to do, and a share of the middle folks too.

Vanishing Without a Trace

I created the myth of "The Animal Man" and have lived that myth by presenting the program to over a million students in the past eighteen years.

Yet, "vanishing without a trace" is very important for me, too. I want the issue to be the animals, conservation and the children's transformation, not me as an individual. The point is not to promote "The Animal Man" but the idea of living in harmony with nature.

So I stay low-key, considering my style to be like that of Ed Sullivan, who was always low-key as he introduced spectacular acts on his television show.

On another level, I am now retiring from that work, handing the reins over to a new animal man, and I have to let go of the need to "be" "The Animal Man." This persona is just a tool to fulfill my vision and must not become a need on my part. In other words, I cannot become addicted to the persona because that will interfere with my flexibility. It will hold me to something I need to let go of. So I must vanish without a trace of regret and fully let go.

Yet the myth that was created still remains—in the memories of the children who saw the program, in their transformation, and now with the new animal man. And, hopefully, there will always be animal people, wandering minstrels telling tales of the earth.

In my T'ai-chi classes, I also tend to act like Ed Sullivan and many of the students wish that were not so. They feel more people would join the school if I were more lively and outgoing.

Yet I want the focus of attention in the classes to be on the students themselves. Otherwise they might be more interested in propping me up as "The Great T'ai-chi Master" than in developing their own skills. I might even become addicted to that persona and start gearing the classes toward enhancing my image rather than to really teaching. Being unobtrusive as a teacher is an insurance against having this happen. This is a form of "vanishing without a trace."

It is said that one's path through life should be like the path of the reflection of the moon over a still lake at midnight. The lake remains undisturbed.

Trusting Yourself

Another aspect of vanishing without a trace is the image of the tunnel, now cleared of personnel and equipment, allowing water to flow through it freely. When you speak or act, the channels have already been opened; you are satisfied with what you have created and now your creative spirit flows through. In other words, after you work on yourself, transform yourself, empty yourself, then you must trust yourself. You must trust that when you act or speak spontaneously, good things will come out.

Vanishing without a trace allows emptiness, which allows the flow of creative energy. The mind then switches roles from that of foreman of the operations to that of chronicler, a describer of the activities of body-mind. Mind describes what is flowing through the tunnel. The mind is no longer judging what may pass through.

The mind is no longer called upon to do tedious work and it can finally relax. The endless spinning of the thinking-mind does, finally, come to an end.

At this point, the water flowing through the tunnel becomes as real as, and more the issue than, the walls of the tunnel. This means that the dynamics of attention become as solid, as real, as perceptible as a chair, a rock or one's body. The pattern of attention—how you as the artist use its colors—becomes the central issue of your life.

The Flow of Creativity

When the advanced student practices healing, it is not merely from an intellectual level. He doesn't check which acupressure point to press by looking it up in a book. Rather, he can feel the flow of energy in the client and the responses of his body to the massage. The masseur's body-mind instructs him as to what to do next and how to do it.

His hands move expertly and his thinking-mind wonders, "How do they know what to do?"

The strange truth is that no matter how far advanced you get, there is always a little part of you that is tied to the old ways of doing things. There is always a part of you that says, "This can't be," even while you see it happening.

But the advanced student doesn't let that old part interfere with his actions. He accepts the old thinking as a permanent part of himself but allows his hands to continue their spontaneous healing "as if" they knew what they were doing.

There is a tendency in T'ai-chi-Ch'uan to do or say the "in" things. For example, it is "in" to say we "play" the Form. T'ai-chi-Ch'uan can become just another thing we study to feel we belong to some group, so we can be approved of.

Looking Inward for the Answers

But this attitude prevents us from looking inside ourselves to find the answers. I attended a festival at the T'ai-chi farm in Warwick, New York, and among the many wonderful people there was Master B. P. Chan. He is a charming and extremely skillful man and very down-to-earth. During one of his seminars he mentioned that if your *body* tells you it can't continue doing some exercise, then stop. Listen to your body.

When I returned from the festival I called a friend of mine who told me she had once gone to a Yoga retreat where the teacher forced her legs into a full lotus position. While she knew that her body was not ready for that, she didn't feel that she could protest because the feeling at this retreat was that you *must* do what the teacher said. The result was that she needed knee surgery.

The point is that T'ai-chi must not become something that earns you "brownie points." It is nothing other than self-discovery, and it requires self-respect.

Think of T'ai-chi as a can opener. You are certainly not as interested in the can opener as in the contents of the can. When I open my cats' can of cat food, they want to examine the can opener and the lid I throw away, but it's only when I present them with the actual food that they are satisfied.

An advanced student is like my cats. He is only satisfied with the actual food. He may look up acupressure points in a book but when it comes to the actual massage, he lets his fingers do the walking.

Transformation through Fighting

I get glimpses that a student is reaching this point, especially in the fighting. The student will strike at me every time my attention wavers even the slightest bit. I can see the punch coming, but I can't get my attention back quickly enough to deal with it, and I get hit. When a student has made such a breakthrough I can sense that I won't be able to get through his defenses. Something has drastically changed.

When he reaches that point, I cannot be tired when I go into the fighting class. I can no longer take the sparring for granted. And this helps me from becoming lazy. The better the students are, the better I get.

It is a surprising feeling to see that a student has caught you at a moment when he knows you won't respond in time. The window of opportunity (when your attention wavers) is just a fraction of a second. When two people are fighting on this level they "hone" their attentions like sharpening two knives by rubbing them against each other. The one who has the more energy that day will wear out the other person's attention by shifting positions, and changing patterns of attention several times per second for many minutes on end. At a certain point, one person's attention will just collapse. Then his partner can strike at liberty.

One of the visible differences between an intermediate and an advanced student is that the intermediate student's facial expression may be very serious. The advanced student smiles a lot as he fights. There is no anger or tension, as he is well within his limitations of endurance both physically and in terms of attention. He can easily evade the partner or glance off his strikes. Fighting for him is not intimidating, it is play.

Many students who have just entered the fighting class remark that our fighting looks like fun. For me personally the fighting is only partially a means of learning self-defense. More importantly, it is an enjoyable sport and a way of being child-like (as opposed to child-ish).

Limitless Potential

The advanced student dreams of what he could get his body and attention to do as if he were in a science fiction or fantasy novel. And then he sets about to do it in real life.

As a simple example, I show a student how to begin a punch with complete looseness, and trigger a pulse of energy from his tan-tien only when his fist first feels contact with the sandbag.

Typically, a student tenses up before or at the beginning of the punch to prepare himself for the resistance of the bag. This initial tensing neutralizes the effectiveness of the punch. Part of the power of the punch comes from the degree of change from looseness to firmness from the time you first contact the partner to the completion of the punch.

It is as if you held two wires, one with a million volts and one with a million-and-one volts. You would only get a shock of one volt—very little. But if you dropped one wire and picked up another with just one volt, the difference between the wires would be 999,999 volts and that would be the end of you.

Yet the idea of coming in with a punch loosely, and firming up while sending a pulse of energy from the tan-tien *only* when you contact the partner or bag, is like a fantasy. How can you react so accurately? The advanced student knows that the human body and attention is capable of almost anything. He never asks, "Can it be done?" He asks, "How can I do it?"

And he dreams up more and more intricate things to do, to test the limits, usually finding out that any limit is just temporary.

Seed-Images

The great trick is creating seeds—images—which do the work for you. These seed-images are the tool of the Taoist magician, the tool of the advanced student.

The seeds contain all that you have learned about T'ai-chi-Ch'uan. Each lesson is related to a symbol, a pattern, whether a visual, feeling or auditory pattern. Each pattern is also related to the yin/yang symbol.

Many of these patterns or images are mentioned throughout this book as well as *Movements of Magic*. Symbols are easier to hold in the mind than entire teachings. They are an extreme simplification of the teaching yet serve to recall all its principles.

The advanced student has taken stock of all these lessons while traveling the path back to his creative spirit.

When he practices the Form or Push Hands or fighting or any practice, he concentrates on the principles relating to his activity in the form of these images or patterns.

The body has been trained in the meaning of each image. The image represents a relationship. For example, one can represent flowing out of the way of a partner's punch. An advanced student's ducking will automatically be triggered by his partner's punch. It is like trying to take a speck of dirt out of a cup of coffee. The speck flows around the spoon simply due to the physical forces involved.

An advanced student's actions are similarly an automatic response to outside actions. The image the student concentrates on controls the relationship between inside and outside.

The student can completely control the relationship to his favor by choosing an appropriate set of images. This control is exercised, of course, by the control of his own behavior and not by attempting to control the other person's behavior.

Politicians and advertisers are well-aware of the power of symbols and use them to control the behavior of the public.

Simplify the Teachings

It is a skill to pack as much teaching into each image as possible. To do this, the student needs to bring the teaching down to its barest, simplest essentials and creatively assign a symbol to each essential. (Remember that this symbol can be a pattern of feeling, not necessarily a visual symbol.) From that, he can assemble a simplified symbol of the whole teaching.

When I was young and before I knew of the yin/yang symbol, I envisioned an image that looked like a vibrating bow tie and then spent many years learning to appreciate its meaning. A symbol can serve as a source of guidance and inspiration. I came to know my symbol as the power that comes from emotional balance.

In the above case, I didn't construct the image (at least not consciously). It popped into my mind and remained there until I felt comfortable that I understood it. Sometimes the smart part of you talks to the dumb part of you in symbols.

The politician is the one who convinces you to take the symbol as the main issue, while the statesman is the one who explains the meaning of the symbol.

You can be a politician in your own life, saying clever things to define your image in a positive way. Or, you can be a statesman, a strategist, and effectively steer your life by learning from each situation you encounter.

The Taoist magician gives up the attempt to be clever and just looks and listens, trying to understand. In fighting, he doesn't prance about but tries to remain still and allow the partner to trigger his responses. Then he comes in with an unending barrage of strikes.

Simplify Your Life

Many people understanding the enormity of what there is to learn in T'ai-chi-Ch'uan, wonder, "Why bother?" Wouldn't it be simpler to just be oblivious?

But as you learn to use the seed-images, your life becomes simpler and more efficient. You learn to respond more quickly and appropriately to situations. At a certain point, the increased ease of living more than makes up for the work you put in.

Haven't we all, after having a discussion, said to ourselves, "I should have said. . . ."? But in the heat of the moment, you couldn't think fast enough. This delay in the ability to react creates a drag on your life. T'ai-chi-Ch'uan eliminates that drag.

The advanced student is at the stage where the benefits to his life far outweigh the effort he puts in. He can call on a seed-image to empower any interaction in his life and truly feels that he, himself, is not doing anything. The seed-images seem to be working on their own. He feels these images are powerful allies. In fact, they can no longer be called "images" because the word "image" implies something that is not really there. Yet the advanced student feels the images as substantially as a rock.

Traditionally, such images are known as spirits, power animals (among American Indians), or energy patterns.

Imitating or Living Life

You know when that break-even point has been passed (where you get back more than you give). Up to that point, many students cannot get the seed-images to do any actual work for them. They know what it would look like if they could, and therefore they imitate what they would look like if they knew how to use seed-images. They still move mechanically and calculate their actions, but in a manner they feel is the "proper way."

Yet you can see that the movements are still not coming from the heart, not from the inside out. They are making themselves move, as a store owner would manipulate the arms and legs of a mannequin into the proper position. They may even feel like a mannequin as they practice.

When they have passed the break-even point, they don't feel like they're doing anything. Their attention is on the seed-images and they are aware of their actions and responses. Yet they don't know how they are able to move. A new mechanism has taken over. It is spontaneous, immediate, effective, playful, relaxed, self-confident and energetic.

I used to feel like I was always on the outside. Even in school, I felt that I was not popular. Yet when I think back, the friends I spent my time with were the very ones I thought of as the most popular in school.

The problem was that I was on the "outside" with regard to myself. I felt robotic, not spontaneous, and I was afraid to speak or act without first going over it in my mind. I didn't trust myself, trust that I would come out with an appropriate comment or action.

This mistrust led me to a stiff, premeditated behavior which took a lot of energy and left me tired. It was not enjoyable to be like this and I compared the lack of joy in myself to what I perceived to be joy in others. I thus felt inadequate at not being able to provide myself with joy.

It was only when I understood the mechanisms of mind and body-mind, and how imitating life is very different from living it, that I could see a way out.

I had been using images in the wrong way. I had an image of how I should act or what I should say, then I made myself do that.

The seed-images come from the relationship of mind and body-mind and the principles of that relationship. These images are the gears that turn the needs of the person into actions, and they are biological in nature, rather than forcefully imposed from the outside.

It is a whole different way of living and the advanced student has made this transition. Whatever work he put into his practice has been amply rewarded. He is no longer a stranger to himself. His attention can gain access to any area and he understands what he sees.

The Metaphors Are Real

When the teacher uses "metaphors," this student knows they are not really metaphors but are direct descriptions of experience. There *is* a "string" holding the head up. It is the "heaven-earth" flow of energy. It is not a metaphor used to trick you to keep your head up. It is a word used to point something out to you that you may not be aware exists.

The focal point of attention *does* ride the crest of the wave of momentum, while the center of attention *does* rest at the tan-tien.

The advanced student goes back to remember all the "metaphors" because now he knows they are really treasures, freely given, keys to freedom handed out to anyone who wants them.

He now takes more seriously what he previously considered to be inconsequential exercises. He knows his T'ai-chi teacher wasn't just talking to fill up class time.

Security in Change

Now he sees that this world we live in is not so finite. It contains endless possibilities of perception. It is difficult to give up the security of a finite, definite order which you can simply take for granted. One of my students who moved to California told me that you don't appreciate the security of walking on solid earth until that security is taken away from you. He said that the frequent earthquakes in California create a deeply disturbing insecurity in a newcomer. You never know if the ground you are walking on will give way.

The advanced T'ai-chi student must give up the security of his perceptual solid ground in order to perceive new things. The ability to feel energy flow changes the relationship of the rest of his senses. His perception of attention patterns allows him to relate to people in new ways.

Now, his power in life must come from what he is willing to give up—his old, sure ways. This dilemma faces us all the time. We can't take advantage of a new opportunity if we cling to our old activities or attitudes.

Doing the Impossible

I tend to go to the other extreme. I think of some outlandish, impossible project to get involved in and go right ahead with it. I enjoy accomplishing the impossible. One part of me says, "How can you do this? It would take so much time and effort. You don't know that much about it and it is almost impossible to do." And another part of me says, "Just do it. Don't worry about what that other part of you is saying. You can do it!"

When I first got my video equipment, I was faced with a dazzling array of buttons and wires. I didn't know how to connect anything, how to use the equipment, let alone the basic principles of editing. The manuals didn't help either. They assume that if you buy equipment like this, you know how to use it.

I made a lot of mistakes but eventually I gained proficiency. When I think back to what I've done and what I'm doing, I'm amazed I had the nerve to think I could create a video production company, basically out of thin air.

I had to give up a lot of the activities and projects so I could immerse myself in this one, and then I had to have solid faith that it would succeed.

The whole project had to be planned strategically—financing, educating myself, promotion, advertising, making connections, working with the printer, with suppliers and customers, creating lines of distribution, reading industry reports on the state and direction of this particular field, etc., etc. I learned to do the artwork for the video sleeves and musical backgrounds for the videos on a synthesizer. Mailings of thousands of leaflets had to go out and telephone calls had to be made to manufacturers of equipment all over the country so I would know which units were the best for my needs.

It was like entering a new culture. My main worry in getting involved with something like this has always been that I would lose my ideals and become a "bottom-line businessman." But I knew that to be effective I had to jump into the business world and trust myself enough to believe I would never lose my ideals.

Now, I use the video business to help teachers of health, exercise and alternative life-styles communicate on a grassroots level with others of like-spirit. By producing a video on their subject, they can reach a world-wide community without going through big-business channels. The communications industry is brought down to a human scale.

Change Is Power

By giving up the security of what I had been doing, I created a valuable service. True security is not found in stagnation but in paying attention to what is going on around you (in this case, noticing that a whole new industry had been born) and being able to change and adapt to the new conditions.

In T'ai-chi-Ch'uan, the skill of paying attention and adapting is taught most notably in Push Hands. Any resistance to the partner results in your getting pushed. There is so much going on all at once that you have no choice but to follow it all and flow with it.

(This is very different from what is known as "Competition Push Hands." In the Push Hands contests, participants don't do much neutralizing, following, or "listening," but try to become as solid as possible and resist the other person. It is a very interesting form of Push Hands, but not the type I refer to in my writings.)

The ability to be aware and to be able to adapt provides the security for the advanced student. You know you will never be caught unprepared. It is a realistic security and one that leads to power. The skill involved in this security consists of knowing what to let go of.

Letting Go Is Power

In Push Hands, we give up resistance. Whenever the partner comes in to us, we give way. This enables our other side to come in to the partner and return his force.

Anatomically, the left hip is attached to the right hip. Many people want to turn in to the partner to push him but don't want to turn their other side away. They think they can resist on the left side and come in on the right side.

Perhaps if there were a hinge at the center of the hips, this could be done. But the advanced student knows that his power to be yang on one side is only equal to his power to be yin on the other side.

Therefore the advanced student will study his life to learn what he can let go of, in order to have even greater power—or at least a healthier kind of power. It is by this process that he now advances in life.

Evaporation from the Eyes

As an example, there is the evaporation from the eyes, and animal staring. Notice the way you look at things. For most people, the eyes "grab" onto what they are looking at. It is as if they reach out through their eyes and grab at what they see. At other times, the eyes are "vacant" because that person's attention is on their thinking-mind and the eyes are on hold. But there is another way of using the eyes, where the eyes can be like pools of water under a waterfall, receiving perception. A person who can achieve this feels attention evaporating off the eyes, like the mist of water created all around the waterfall.

That evaporation is a letting-go of attention, a letting-go of the grabbing. While your attention still "fills up" the scene before you, there is no grabbing involved. The attention evaporates to fill up your world.

When two such people interact, the evaporating attention interacts as in Push Hands. When you work with animals, you will feel that each species has its own characteristic style of interaction of attention. You can learn the style of each and then interact with people in the same way. The results are very powerful—too powerful, in fact, to be used indiscriminately. On the other hand, it can be used for positive purposes such as healing.

The point is that, in order to allow your pattern of attention to match the style of another animal, you must temporarily give up your own "style." This requires a very intimate giving-up. You are letting go of the very basis of your behavior as an individual, to gain fluidity.

Some advanced students decide to live ascetic lives—to give up material and sensual fulfillment. Yet it is even more difficult to live in the "real" world and live a normal life and still develop the "art of letting go." I don't think the ascetics ever really develop this art. They just imitate doing so.

Imperfection Is Power

One very important form of letting go is forgiving. You forgive yourself for whatever negative feelings you have about yourself. Then you forgive other people for not meeting up to your great expectations. Sometimes having negative opinions about people can be an addiction. I have heard many discussions of groups of people centered around why this one and that one are "no good." That seemed to be the only way they could feel good about themselves, as if they were the models of perfection. Accepting yourself as imperfect but one who can learn, can be a great change for some people. They must forgive their imperfections.

This is driven home in the fighting. The first few injuries you receive are devastating. Then, you get used to your bruises, jammed fingers, sprains, etc.

The idea of your body having been damaged—made imperfect—is worse than the actual pain you receive. Yet you must give up the need to be perfect or you would never agree to learn fighting. This is why we start out the class by punching each other lightly in the face twenty or thirty times (with gloves). It gets us over the fear of getting hit.

The need for perfection is related to the desire to get everything you want, as a child. "I want" is the child's operative phrase, whether it's food, toys or your attention. Living strategically is the opposite of living from "I want."

I used to travel on the Long Island Railroad and watch people play cards. Someone explained to me that he would purposefully let the other players take some of his cards so he could figure out what cards they had in their hand. Then he would win the rest of the other people's cards. He played cards strategically. He didn't just say, "I want as many cards as I can get," but knew how to give some cards up in order to win the game.

Behavioral Blindness

Many fighting students are very aggressive. They come in blindly and just try to throw as many punches as possible. They want to hit me. So I encourage their aggression by moving backwards so they will keep coming in. Meanwhile, I keep hitting them in the head while ducking their strikes. They are so excited about coming in that they don't notice they are getting the bad end of the deal.

Then I say to them, "Haven't you noticed that you're getting hit in the head a lot?"

Have you, the reader, ever felt that way as you go through life?

Such a student has to give up his blind raging rush to hit me, and really learn sparring strategically. He has to pay attention to what was going on around him to see what is working and what isn't.

As a child, I was afraid of falling into habit patterns and losing my awareness. So I played a little game. At odd times, here and there, I would perform some motions which had no relation to anything that was going on at the time.

(I did this while alone.) This was to introduce into my life activities unconnected to any pattern of behavior I may have developed.

It was like the ball-bearing that is in spray cans of paint and allows you to better shake up the paint. These arbitrary motions helped keep my life free of "lumps" of behavior.

Sometimes, in the mad rush to live our lives, we lose our awareness, fall into "secure" behavior patterns and then wonder why we are getting hit in the head so much.

Letting Go of Safety Can Be Power

The beginning student will attempt to keep his head away from the partner, in sparring, while trying to get his punch into the partner. He tries to separate these two parts of his body, one going one way and one the other, and thinks he can be efficient. This impossible behavior does not result in security or efficiency but in absurdity, and he tends to get hit a lot. The advanced student puts his head right into the middle of the action but keeps it moving, weaving in and out of the partner's strikes, as he delivers his own strikes to the partner. When he punches, he brings his head and his awareness with him.

Teaching T'ai-chi

You learn to appreciate the devastating result of this loss of awareness when you begin to teach T'ai-chi-Ch'uan to others. The advanced student learns to become a teacher.

By the word "teacher," I don't mean an instructor. Even beginning students can instruct those who know less.

A teacher can see inside the student and know how to reconnect him to himself. A teacher can lead the student to his own spirit but not interfere with that spirit.

By seeing how far some students have strayed from their own spirits, the advanced student will remember how much T'ai-chi has done for him. He can appreciate how teaching a particular aspect of the Form will bring a student closer to his spirit in a particular way.

Spontaneity is an example. When a student's actions do not emanate from his spirit, he must think, "How can I respond in such a way as to create the proper impression of who I am?" Or, "How can I react to control that person?" When you give up these desires, you are free, because you just respond to enjoy the moment and to be efficient.

To enjoy the moment, you can just be yourself. To be efficient, you can act the way you are biologically designed to act. Each is effortless. A teacher will show a student how to be effortless in his movements and will see the student struggle to become effortless. That is, of course, a contradiction in terms and lies at the root of the student's problem.

Becoming effortless is a process of letting go, not of gaining something. A teacher encourages the student to let go of pushing himself through life or through the Form. The teacher then waits to see what kind of spirit emerges when the heavy lid of self-conscious behavior is lifted.

Think of the teacher as a raccoon, which sneaks around at night, breaking open your food containers—lifting the heavy rocks you placed on your box of food and even deftly unscrewing the bottles. In the same way, the teacher tries to unscrew the containers in which your spirit is packed away. He can smell your spirit from a mile away and wants to release it.

The Form—Diagnosis for Healing

As the teacher goes through this process with each student, he notices qualities of the Form associated with particular problems in getting the student back to his spirit. He can see that when the student makes progress in being spontaneous, his Form changes in a particular way.

The Form, then, becomes a diagnostic tool to understand the degree of spontaneity of the student, his connection to his spirit, and the relationship of mind and body-mind.

Since such inner relationships lie at the heart of our health, the Form can be a diagnostic tool for a healer and a T'ai-chi teacher is, of course, a kind of healer. If something stands in the way of our spontaneity, some fear of what that spontaneity will lead to, our power will be trapped. The creative energy that flows through us is the same as the healing energy.

When we are spontaneous, we don't fear what we will do. We know there is no violence or damaging potential within us (after much T'ai-chi training). We know this because we can see ourselves. We can see what's in there.

Then we can relax and let ourselves live. But if we are always on edge, fearful of what we really are deep down inside, we will be blocking our normal, spontaneous functioning—not only on a social level, but on a medical level as well.

That attitude of holding ourselves in check, out of fear, cannot be limited to just a social level. It usually affects all aspects of our lives.

So, to be creative, to let it all come through, to know and trust what is inside you, is a very healing process. That's what I mean by saying that the creative energy and the healing energy are one and the same.

T'ai-chi-Ch'uan is this kind of healing process and the Form is the doorway into it. The teacher uses it as a diagnostic tool. Having gone through such a process himself, the teacher can know the student's situation. He may notice that the student's posture is off in a certain way or his movements are awkward in a certain way.

By imagining himself practicing in that incorrect way, the teacher can get an appreciation for what state the student is in, to be doing such things. He can then build a more detailed picture of the student's inner situation, the student's fears, tensions, resistances, etc., and better know how to get him out of his predicament.

Crafting a Path to Freedom

The teacher will use corrections in the Form, Push Hands, etc., to create a path out of that predicament. This is what separates a teacher from an instructor. Their corrections may be the same (sink the hips, relax those shoulders), but the teacher is guiding his student down a path to freedom while the instructor is just telling the student what to do.

His particular style of creating such paths is a legacy which he passes to his students. They will remember the nature of his guidance and use that as a basis for their own healing when they become teachers. At the same time, the teacher has to encourage each student to create his own style of healing according to his own nature.

Each teacher also performs the Form and does Push Hands slightly differently. Such differences reflect the different styles of healing and allow these exercises to become physical records of the teacher's healing style. The different styles of the Form are but many different pathways back to one's own spirit.

In your first experiences as a teacher, you must remember that you traversed only one pathway, appropriate for your situation. It is a mistake to think everyone must take that same pathway. So when you begin to teach, you are not a craftsman. You can only make one kind of product, one kind of path.

The craftsman-teacher must craft a path appropriate for each student's needs. The beginning teacher must learn the tools of his craft, the materials, and what kinds of products can be made.

So when he begins to teach, he is truly beginning to learn T'ai-chi. He learns in how many ways we have strayed from our spirit and how this loss of awareness has devastated us.

His craft is similar to a jungle guide. All the student can see are dense vines and trees. But the guide can sense the right direction and is aware of all the animals lurking behind the bushes. Each journey through the jungle is different. Yet the jungle itself is part of him. It is his territory, his life.

The T'ai-chi teacher is a guide, leading the student through the jungle back to his own spirit. And as he guides, he continues to discover new paths and creatures.

He is not just a T'ai-chi student or teacher. He is a magical creature of the forest.

EPILOGUE

DREAM EAGLE

Who ever rode an eagle to the top of Mount Kelo?

The Eaglemaster stroked the long brown feathers of Billy's mount. His tiny smile, the twinkle in his eye, told Billy that it was time to escape.

The Great Eagle soared through warm winds, the boy clinging to its fluffy neck.

"We have flown to the top of smaller mountains many times," the boy whispered to his dream-eagle, "but today we shall fly higher than ever!"

Great Eagle was just as anxious to visit Billy's world. Together they trained for many years just for this day. Eagle spiraled down the valley again and again to gain speed. Tidal waves of wind tugged at Billy's grip as they headed straight for the Wall of Dreams.

Crash! Tumbling rocks and a gaping hole.

The two had escaped into the world of those-who-are-awake. But Dream Eagle began to fall.

"Everything is so heavy here," it shouted. "I'm being pulled down, down."

The pair thudded to a landing. "Eagle! What is wrong? You have always flown so high!"

But Dream Eagle could not support the weight of a waking boy. "What are we to do?" they both thought.

A bright orange sun sank behind Mount Kelo. Orange, purple and black drifted in the sky.

Boy and eagle sat below the mountain on a large rock. They were to live together in the world of those-who-are-awake. Eagle and boy had trained for many years behind the Wall of Dreams where there was no weight. Now, how could they fly to the mountaintops together?

The eagle knew how. "I can only bring your dream body to the top of the mountain. Your heavy part must stay on the ground. But I promise to carry your light body to every mountaintop on this earth."

Billy lived many years. Each night when he dreamed, the boy visited a different mountaintop. And when he grew old and died, when he left his heavy body to the creatures of the earth, Billy flew up to Mount Kelo on Eagle's back.

Just before reaching the top, a huge gust of wind blew Billy off. "Help me, Eagle!" he shouted.

But Eagle kept flying up to the mountaintop. It shouted back, "You do not need me to fly anymore."

And that was true, for Billy could now fly on his own and flew to the top of the mountain.

"Why didn't you tell me I could fly before?" he asked Eagle. "I would have joined you sooner."

"That could not be," his friend answered. "All this time I have been preparing you to become a dream boy so you can fly to new worlds. You have been teaching me to become a waking eagle so I can explore this one. We have been good friends and taught each other much. Now we must part."

A dream drifted off above the clouds to new worlds. And another dream flew below the clouds, a vision for all to see.